UNSTOPPABLE

UNSTOPPABLE

True Stories of Amazing Bionic Animals

NANCY FURSTINGER

Houghton Mifflin Harcourt
Boston   New York

www.hmhco.com
The text type was set in Century Old Style Std.
The display type was set in Proxima Nova.

Library of Congress Cataloging-in-Publication Data

Names: Furstinger, Nancy, author.
Title: Unstoppable : true stories of amazing bionic animals / Nancy Furstinger.
Description: Boston ; New York : Houghton Mifflin Harcourt, [2017]
Identifiers: LCCN 2016038370 | ISBN 9780544879669 (hardcover)
Subjects: LCSH: Veterinary surgery—Juvenile literature. | Domestic animals—Surgery—Juvenile literature. | Artificial limbs—Juvenile literature. | Prosthesis—Juvenile literature. | Bionics—Juvenile literature.
Classification: LCC SF911 .F96 2017 | DDC 636.089/7—dc23
LC record available at https://lccn.loc.gov/2016038370

Manufactured in China
SCP 10 9 8 7 6 5 4 3 2
4500704201

CONTENTS

INTRODUCTION

"Attitude is a little thing that makes a big difference."

—Winston Churchill

All the animals in this book inspire us with their gumption. They have strong will and determination, proving that it's possible to conquer life's obstacles. The wild and domestic species profiled from around the world don't let their limitations get in the way of living. These uplifting stories show that physically challenged animals can adapt to almost any circumstance. They celebrate what it means to be considered "different," and they demonstrate that there's no such thing as normal. Behind each animal is a team of dedicated rescuers, compassionate veterinarians, and orthotic and prosthetic professionals armed with cutting-edge technological advances.

They've created custom-designed wheelchairs and prosthetic limbs, tails, fins, flippers, and beaks to replace missing or nonworking body parts. In the process, they've given these specially abled animals a second chance by improving their mobility and their quality of life.

Many of these medical miracles have crossed over from human medicine, revolutionizing veterinary medicine. Conversely, some animal medical advances are benefiting humans. Sharing progressive technologies can be mutually beneficial to all species!

Today, pioneering innovations are helping our two- and four-legged animal and human friends. Sounding as if it is straight out of science fiction, 3D printing allows researchers to precisely design and produce bionic body parts. Another fusion of technologies offering options for human and animal amputees is the science of osseointegration. This alternative way of attaching a prosthetic limb uses a titanium implant, inserted into the residual limb, which gradually becomes part of the bone.

Amazing inventions, such as robotic prosthetic limbs controlled by thought, are evolving at a rapid pace. More incredible discoveries are on the way, making anything possible for bionic animals of the future!

THE COMEBACK

ANIMALS

ALBIE, FELIX, AND FAWN

Finding Strength in Their Differences at a Farm Sanctuary

Follow Rescue Road as it winds through Woodstock Farm Sanctuary in High Falls, New York, and you might spot a cow sporting a pink leg brace, a goat cruising around in a wheelchair, and a sheep cavorting with his flock on a prosthetic leg. Nothing, not even a missing limb, stops the animals who live on this storybook farm from savoring life without limitations. Here, the tales have happy endings; in fact, the close to 350 animals who live at the 150-acre sanctuary have all triumphed over sad beginnings.

Albie, a shaggy white goat named after the compassionate philosopher and humanitarian Albert Schweitzer, was just a kid when he escaped from a slaughterhouse in New York City. Gashes etched Albie's legs. Someone had hogtied the tiny goat,

JENNY BROWN, COFOUNDER OF THE WOODSTOCK FARM SANCTUARY, SCRATCHES DEVLIN, A RAM WHO SURVIVED A HUGE HOARDING CASE IN PENNSYLVANIA.

binding together all four of his legs so that he could be transported to slaughter.

Then Albie got his second chance. Police grabbed the roaming goat and took him to a city animal shelter. The staff knew just whom to contact: Jenny Brown. If animals are the stars at Woodstock Farm Sanctuary, Jenny is their leading lady. The sanctuary cofounder started welcoming animals to her haven in 2004. Along with her husband, Doug Abel, and their staff and volunteers, Jenny rescues, rehabilitates, and cares for farm animal refugees.

Jenny nursed Albie back to health, but his front leg refused

ALBIE RELAXES IN THE GOAT AND SHEEP BARN.

to heal. The tight binding had cut off the goat's circulation, causing his leg to become badly infected and his hoof to crumble. Jenny made the difficult decision to have his leg amputated just above the knee. Now two amputees lived at the sanctuary: Albie and Jenny.

At the age of ten, Jenny lost part of her right leg due to bone cancer. She wears a prosthetic leg that hasn't stopped her from actively running her sanctuary. "It's a leg, not a lobotomy," Jenny emphasizes as we walk through the farm with her three-legged dog, Sophie, racing ahead of us. Her prosthetic leg changed her life, and she wanted nothing less for Albie. "I know the challenges that can come from missing a limb, and I also know what's available in technology that could help improve his life," she said.

So Jenny took a bold step and asked her own certified prosthetist, Erik J. Tompkins, to craft a leg for the little goat. A prosthetist is a health professional who is specially trained to work with prosthetics, but even Erik admitted that he wasn't an expert on fitting *animals* with artificial limbs, and the task was even more complicated because goats have hooves. "It's like they're always wearing little high-heeled shoes," said Jenny, adding that this makes their skeletons different from those of most animals.

Six months after Albie entered the sanctuary, he was walking on four legs! But the active young goat continued to face challenges. As Albie grew, he went through a series of artificial legs, but he managed to wiggle out of each one of them. Because the goat's amputation was above the knee, nothing kept the leg on—not harnesses, straps, or special liners. Would Albie have to go back to hobbling around on three legs? Some animals, such as dogs, can maneuver on three legs; however, goats aren't anatomically designed to adjust to life with a missing limb. Without the use of four legs, Albie's mobility would be challenged, probably causing damage to his spine and his opposite leg. What could be done for him?

As Dr. Tompkins and Jenny brainstormed different ideas to solve Albie's dilemma, Woodstock Farm Sanctuary started welcoming other physically challenged animals. Like Albie, another baby animal being raised for slaughter desperately

needed rescuing. A predator snuck into a sheep farm, grabbed a young lamb, and chewed off part of his left rear leg. The lamb escaped but received no vet care, as he was destined for the dinner table. Fortunately, a farm worker brought the lamb, whom Jenny named Felix, to the sanctuary. Jenny and Doug bottle-fed the lamb, and he lived in their house as he healed.

Later, the barnyard flock greeted Felix as he limped around on three legs. This Katahdin lamb sports a coat of hair instead of fleece. The Katahdin breed was developed in Maine as "hair sheep" who, because they were intended for meat, would not require annual shearing as woolly breeds do. As Felix grew, he too needed a prosthetic leg. His first leg, created by a specialist in Virginia who makes prosthetics for animals with amputations, wore down after a few years. It was time to go high-tech!

After a cofounder of the Hudson Valley Advanced Manufacturing Center at the nearby State University of New York at New Paltz toured the sanctuary, he thought Felix would be a good candidate for a 3D-printed prosthetic leg. A team assembled to make this a reality: Jenny, her prosthetist Erik, manufacturing center technicians, a vet at Cornell University, and a biology major at the university. They used the school's 3D printer to create a lightweight leg out of the same plastic used to manufacture Lego blocks. The state-of-the-art prosthetic "allows him to

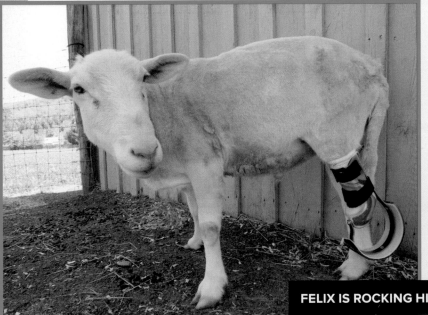

FELIX IS ROCKING HIS FIRST PROSTHETIC LIMB.

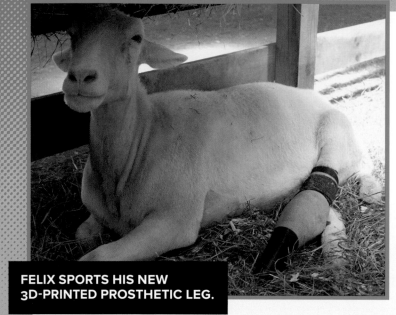

FELIX SPORTS HIS NEW 3D-PRINTED PROSTHETIC LEG.

move with a normal gait and run and play and keep up with the other sheep," said Jenny.

• • • •

When a Jersey dairy cow gave birth, her calf didn't take her first breath in cozy straw bedding. Instead, the calf fell into a concrete manure pit behind the milking stall where her mother was chained. The newborn smashed her front left knee. A local woman adopted the calf, called Fawn, as a pet, but the calf's fractured and infected knee never healed.

Fawn grew and grew until her healthy right front leg was unable to support her increasing weight. The young cow's legs started bowing outward at the knees, and she soon was unable to stand up. Fawn resorted to moving around with great difficulty, balancing on her front knees. At that point Fawn's rescuer reached out to Woodstock Farm Sanctuary. Could they help?

Jenny brought Fawn to the experts at Cornell Veterinary Hospital in central New York. She braced herself for the possibility that the cow would never walk again. Surprisingly, the head surgeon believed he could restore Fawn's ability to walk normally. He and his team operated on both of Fawn's front legs, which Jenny described as being "bent horribly." The team removed a row of bones that was damaged and then glued together the remaining bones.

Although the surgery was successful, Fawn still faced an uphill struggle. Her left front leg was fused at the knee, so it couldn't bend, and it was also two inches shorter than her right front leg, which bowed outward. Fawn tried to compensate by making her shoulders level when she attempted to walk, which was very hard on her. Ronnie N. Graves, a prosthetist specializing in large animals, took a cast to make a model of both of Fawn's front legs. Then he used the models to create a pair of pink clamshell-type braces that helped the cow "get around so well

that everyone at the sanctuary has to really keep an eye on her," Ronnie said.

Would everyone at Woodstock Farm Sanctuary also have to keep an eagle eye on Albie? He kept kicking off every leg designed for him—seven in all, each time leading his caregivers on a wild goat chase to find the prosthetics before they vanished in the pasture or the straw bedding. What could be done to help Albie move forward? With a variety of prosthetic options for both humans and animals being used around the world, a solution *had* to be on the horizon.

When Jennie puts the braces on Fawn, Fawn gets excited and earns the nickname "Happy Cow."

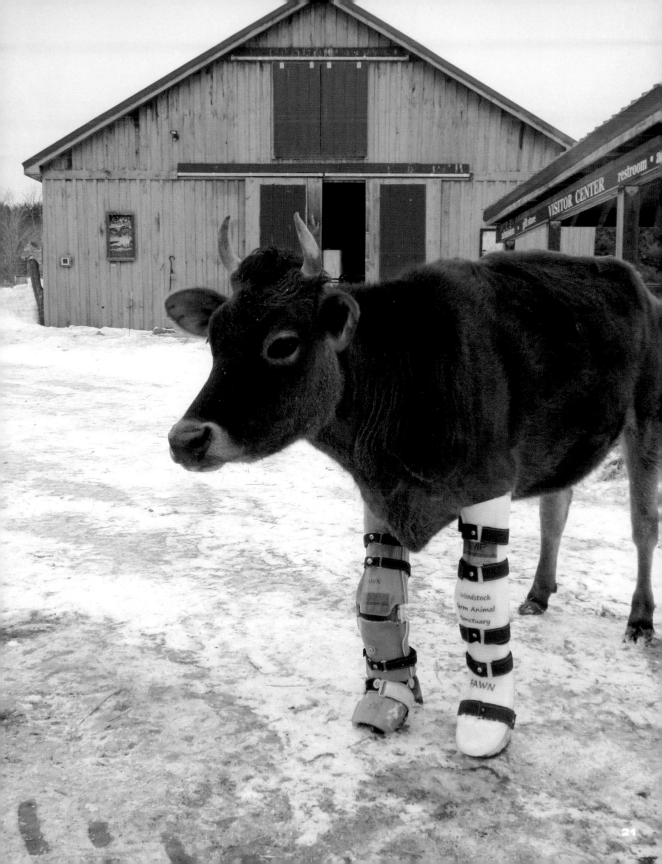

TACKLING A TRICKY CHALLENGE

Erik J. Tompkins combines athletic and artistic skills to design prosthetics primarily for people. Both talents proved handy when he evaluated his new patient: a goat named Albie. The goat wasn't Erik's first four-legged client. He had fitted a twenty-five-year-old horse with a brace to correct a front leg that was four inches shorter than the other three legs. Erik needed strength and endurance to cast the horse's leg, along with inventiveness to create the brace.

When the certified prosthetist got a phone call from his human client, Jenny Brown, asking if he'd design a leg for a rescued goat at Woodstock Farm Sanctuary, he tackled the challenge. "I knew I could figure it out and apply what I've learned with human patients," said Erik, adding that he's fitted some "complicated humans" in his twenty-four years of practice.

Jenny's background training at Farm Sanctuary in Watkins Glen, New York, not only gave her the essential experience to start a sanctuary of her own, but it also led to her collaborating with Erik. She offered Erik input on designing Albie's leg based on a goat at Farm Sanctuary that she had taken care of there. "That goat had a deformed leg that required amputation, so she used a prosthetic leg, too," Jenny said.

Now it was Albie's turn. Once the goat's stump healed, Erik created a cast and built a prototype prosthetic leg, which he described as "an

old-fashioned peg leg" similar to the one that Captain Hook wore. Albie's new leg had a soft interior and a tough fiberglass exterior that allowed the goat to bear weight. Instead of a cloven hoof, Eric substituted a rubber cane tip to "cushion the step and help with traction."

These days Erik specializes in more cutting-edge prosthetics. As a member of the Upper Limb Prosthetic Society, he is fitting advanced silicone sockets that have pattern recognition and are able to control powered elbows and multiple articulating hands such as the i-limb and Michelangelo hands. These devices have electrically positionable thumbs, seven different grips, and flexible wrists. Perhaps someday he will be testing out a brain-controlled bionic limb for an animal patient.

ALLISON

Paddling in New Directions with Her Ninja Suit

When Allison's caregivers first attached her ninja suit, which was topped with a prosthetic dorsal fin, the green sea turtle experienced an *aha* moment. There was an "immediate transformation," recalled Jeff George, the executive director of Sea Turtle, Inc., a sea turtle rescue center on South Padre Island, Texas. "You could see it; she knew she could swim without struggling."

Allison had been able to swim only in counterclockwise circles when she arrived at the center from the island's beach. The palm-size sea turtle bumped her head against the bottom of her tank to propel to the surface so she could breathe. Since green sea turtles can live well over a hundred years, the staff won-

ALLISON HAS ONE REMAINING FLIPPER AFTER SURVIVING A PREDATOR ATTACK IN 2005.

dered whether Allison, only two at the time, would be doomed to swimming in circles in her tank for a century.

All sea turtles battle natural predators before they even hatch, and at first Allison managed to dodge her enemies. She emerged from her egg and scrambled on in the dangerous journey from nest to sea. But then her luck ran out. A shark attacked her, and tourists found her stranded, missing three out of her four flippers.

Sea turtles with three flippers can be released back into the sea. Those with two must live in a sanctuary as permanent residents. But a sea turtle with only one flipper has a slim chance of survival anywhere. Flippers are vital to sea turtles "because they help them get around in their environment," explained Sea Turtle, Inc.'s Megan Chilcutt. "The front flippers of a sea turtle are used for power as they swim, and the back flippers are used for steering." With her single right front flipper, Allison could only make tight left-hand turns as she swam.

Yet this one-flippered sea turtle proved to be a fighter. Once she healed, the rescue center decided to fit Allison with a prosthetic flipper, something that had never before been attempted. A team made up of a veterinarian, a plastic surgeon for humans, and a dentist from the University of Texas Dental Branch created a silicone flipper to attach to Allison's front left nub. This cooperation between veterinary and human doctors has led to medical advances for different species. Unfortunately, the stump was too short to hold the fake flipper, and everything fell off within seconds.

Watching this process, a young intern at the rescue center had an *a-ha* mo-

WITH ONLY ONE FLIPPER, ALLISON SWIMS IN TIGHT CIRCLES.

TOM WILSON, CREATOR OF ALLISON'S FIRST "NINJA SUIT," BEAMS AS THE SEA TURTLE SWIMS IN HER TANK.

ment of his own. Tom Wilson thought about how he paddled his canoe to cut a straight path through the water. The long keel of the canoe allowed it to move in a straight line even when Tom paddled it from only one side. Could a design like this offer a solution to help Allison?

Tom used twenty-five dollars worth of supplies to cobble together Allison's first "ninja suit," as her handlers call it. The intern created a homemade wetsuit with a plywood rudder held on by metal clamps. The design worked! Allison could change directions by varying the strokes of the one flipper the shark hadn't chomped

THE FIN ON ALLISON'S HIGH-TECH SWIMSUIT ALLOWS HER TO SWIM STRAIGHT.

NOW ALLISON CAN SWIM IN ANY DIRECTION THAT SHE WANTS!

on. Ironically, the back fin of her suit, which acts as a rudder and allows her to swim straight, resembles the tall dorsal fin of a shark.

Allison now wears the sixth version of her prosthesis. Scientists needed to turtle-proof the space-age swimsuit after her tank-mate crunched down on it. They created a high-tech version using carbon fiber and, for tight clamping and quick release, attached it with a ratcheting system that came off a snowboard.

The first time that Allison dove, using her prosthetic flipper to graze on an underwater salad bar, her audience wept for joy. As she grows—she could weigh up to 450 pounds—she'll be testing out newer versions that will allow her to sail smoothly through the water and enable her to enjoy a long, long life.

Sea turtles cannot pull their heads or flippers into their shells to evade predators above and below the water.

BRUTUS

High-Stepping on Four Faux Paws

he rottweiler raised his inquisitive rust-colored eyebrows as he waited to go outside. But first Brutus needed a little assistance from his best pal. Laura Aquilina strapped on four bionic paws as the patient pooch stretched out on his side. Then Brutus pranced down the street to sniff out the day's next adventure.

LAURA AQUILINA STRAPS ON BRUTUS'S NEW PAWS.

A whole new world of mobility opened up for this quadruple amputee once he received those four prosthetic limbs. Before, Brutus hobbled around indoors on his "little peg legs," but walking outside was painful, said Laura. It even hurt to walk on grass, as he lacked any extra cushioning.

WITHOUT HIS FOUR FAUX PAWS, BRUTUS FACES LOCOMOTIVE CHALLENGES.

Brutus started life with all four paws. When a backyard breeder in Colorado left the puppy outside in freezing temperatures, the result was an awful case of frostbite. Instead of seeking veterinary care, the breeder amputated Brutus's paws. Backyard breeders typically breed animals for profit without providing adequate standards of care. Later, the breeder gave the maimed puppy to a family, but as the rottweiler grew, his physical challenges escalated and the family sought a foster home that could tend to the pup's special needs.

Laura Aquilina and her husband fostered Brutus and ended up adopting him. "It finally dawned on us that we were looking for what he had already found: a family committed to working with him physically and behaviorally, and able to care for his medical needs."

Brutus's new family watched their determined dog face locomotive challenges. Without paws and toe pads, he had lost his sensitivity to feeling the ground. Although Laura noted that Brutus "adapted to his limb differences and found the most comfortable way to walk around," he was walking on skin and bone and couldn't get a grip on hard, smooth surfaces. "The biggest challenge has been for us to find creative solutions to aid and increase his mobility," she added.

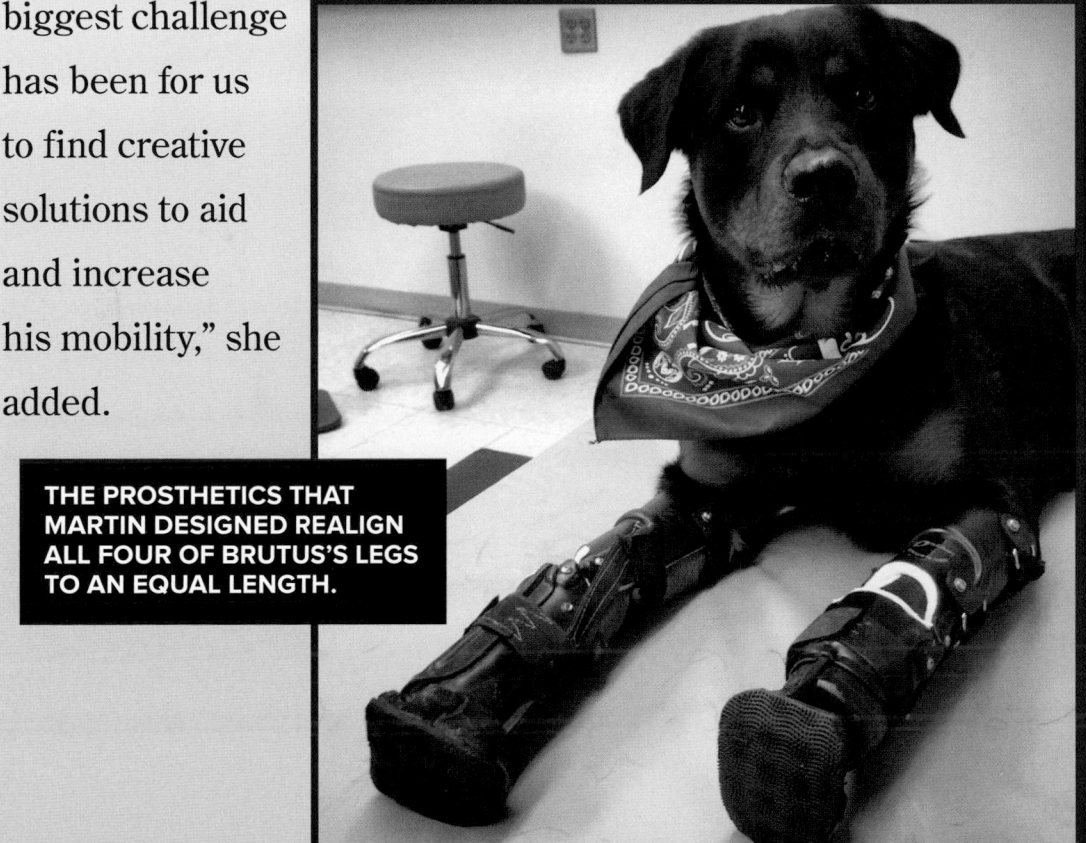

THE PROSTHETICS THAT MARTIN DESIGNED REALIGN ALL FOUR OF BRUTUS'S LEGS TO AN EQUAL LENGTH.

Then the woman who coordinated Brutus's rescue, Laura Ornelas, told his new family that someone right in nearby Denver could tackle that challenge—Martin Kaufmann, the founder and owner of OrthoPets, a company that makes replacement limbs for animals. By coincidence, Martin had crafted a solution to help another dog who was missing his paws. Naki'o, a stray puppy who had also lost his paws to frostbite, became the world's first dog to receive four prosthetic paws. "Naki'o's case showed us that our canine friends are more adaptable than we think," Martin said. Only a few years ago this innovative technology would have been unimaginable, but thankfully, veterinary science has been advancing by leaps.

NAKI'O IS THE WORLD'S FIRST DOG TO BE FITTED WITH FOUR BIONIC PAWS.

Now it was Brutus's turn. After a crowd-funding project dubbed "Better Paws for Brutus" raised more than $12,000, the pooch was fitted for his new set of faux paws. Martin designed the prosthetics with three purposes. First and most important, they would pad and protect Brutus's existing limbs. The new paws would also support his wrist joints, which were collapsing downward "like a badly sprained ankle joint, making each step painful and unstable." Finally, the prosthetics would realign each leg to an equal length. "Just image sitting on a chair that had four different leg lengths," explained Martin. "The result would be very difficult for you to balance on your seat, causing fatigue and reduction in activity."

After surgery, Brutus was off and running—or as close to it as possible. Laura admitted that her dog's awkward, high-stepping gait "is not always pretty," but after physical therapy, which included balancing activities, stretching, and underwater treadmills, Brutus can race across the yard to chase squirrels.

A lack of paws hasn't slowed Brutus down: he enjoys swimming, paddleboarding, and K9 Nose Work.

A 3,000-YEAR-OLD TOE

Although many modern prosthetics appear to have stepped out of the future, most bionics—such as prosthetic limbs, running blades, and robotic arms controlled by brainpower—can actually be traced back to a fake big toe discovered on an Egyptian mummy. The primitive wood and leather toe dates possibly as far back as 950 B.C. and is believed to be the earliest prosthesis. Dubbed the "Cairo Toe," this digit was unearthed from a mummy's tomb near the ancient city of Thebes.

The toe looks lifelike, right down to its curved toenail. But the Cairo Toe went beyond cosmetic: it was designed to be functional to its wearer by aiding mobility. The toe was jointed in three spots and contained holes for lacings to help its owner, a priest's daughter, walk like an Egyptian, comfortably, while wearing her sandals.

CHHOUK

Putting His Best Foot Forward

An endangered baby Asian elephant stumbled through the remote Cambodian forest, separated from his mother, starving, and scared. As if that weren't enough, he was missing the bottom portion of his left front leg.

No more than a year old, the young male was facing enormous challenges when an elephant patrol discovered him. His severe foot injury, sustained from a poacher's snare, had caused the elephant's stump to become swollen and infected. But he refused to accept help, turning up his trunk at the food his rescuers tried to feed him and acting aggressively.

Before the elephant's situation had a chance to become worse, the Cambodian Forestry Administration reached out to

Nick Marx, the wildlife programs director for an international nonprofit organization called Wildlife Alliance. Nick and his team raced across the country, where they hand-fed the elephant and slept next to him in hammocks, spending two weeks in the jungle to gain his trust. They knew that the baby elephant, whom they named Chhouk (which means "lotus flower" in Cambodian), would never survive on his own, so together they set out on a grueling twenty-six-hour journey to get him to the Phnom Tamao Wildlife Rescue Center, around three hundred miles away. Chhouk was initially fretful on one treacherous ten-mile stretch, but he calmed down when fed turnips and sugar cane.

At the rescue center, Wildlife Alliance veterinarians removed almost five inches of infected tissue and bone from Chhouk's leg. The pachyderm surprised everyone by surviving, but he wasn't out of danger. Balancing his bulky body on three feet had taken its toll. Chhouk was off-balance. The damage caused by his missing

CHHOUK'S LIFE CHANGES RADICALLY ONCE HE IS FITTED WITH A PROSTHETIC FOOT.

foot threatened his spine and hips, and he was at risk of developing bone deformities as he grew.

There was only one solution: Chhouk needed to be fitted with a prosthetic foot. The Cambodian School of Prosthetics and Orthotics sprang into action. A team took a mold of the elephant's limb and filled it with plaster to create a cast. Then they made a foam inner socket, wrapped it with strong plastic, and added rubber edging to the bottom of the foot to cushion it.

CHHOUK SPLASHES ATOP HIS CONSTANT COMPANION, LUCKY.

CHHOUK CAN BE FITTED QUICKLY FOR HIS NEW PROSTHETIC FOOT IN A SPECIAL ENCLOSURE AS LONG AS HE RECEIVES BANANA BRIBES.

According to Wildlife Alliance, "Immediately after being fitted with the foot, Chhouk's issues improved rapidly." Once he gained his balance, the elephant's life "changed radically," allowing him to walk for longer distances in the forest and to swim in the lake.

At age ten, Chhouk continues to grow—he may weigh up to 5.5 tons as a full-grown bull elephant. Every six months he receives a newly designed prosthetic foot. Chhouk never needs

CHHOUK AND HIS PAL LUCKY ENJOY RAMBLING THROUGH THE FOREST.

to be sedated; after he enters a special $30,000 enclosure that contains protective barriers his keepers can reach through, it takes thirty seconds to fit his new foot. "As long as he receives a steady stream of bananas, he is content to let the team and his keepers work around his feet," Nick said.

Along with a new foot and a safe habitat free from poaching dangers, Chhouk gained a new friend. Lucky, an older female elephant also rescued as a baby, adopted him like a protective big sister. The two pachyderms share an enclosure and wallow together in the mud next to their pool. "Lucky also likes to remove Chhouk's prosthetic and play with it, causing many more repairs to be made between new shoes," according to Wildlife Alliance.

In addition to Asian elephants, the Phnom Tamao Center has rescued illegally traded wildlife, including tigers, clouded leopards, gibbons, and Malayan sun bears.

CHRIS P. BACON

Hamming It Up as an Internet Star

The piglet grunted with displeasure while bucking his backside. Chris P. Bacon couldn't get the hang of the strange contraption attached to his rear. But the tiny potbelly pig had a determined spirit and soon started rolling around on his new wheels. His video, *Pig in Wheelchair,* went viral with nearly two and a half million views. At only ten days old, Chris P. Bacon already was a ham!

Fortunately for Chris, the veterinarian who rescued him back in January 2013 was equally pigheaded. Dr. Len Lucero was working at an animal clinic when a woman dropped off a newborn piglet to be euthanized because his hind legs were malformed. But Len refused. The vet examined the pig and discovered that he had been "born with rear legs that were not fully formed and could not support his weight or provide him with mobility." Otherwise the piglet was perfectly healthy. His great big grin quickly captivated Len, who decided to adopt him "so he could have a chance at life."

The vet named the plucky pig Chris P. Bacon after a character in a video game. As soon as Chris arrived at Len's Florida home, he started exploring the family room by scooting around using his front feet. Len grabbed a box of his son's snap-together toys and swiftly constructed a wheelchair for his one-pound pig. Then Len harnessed his new pet into the device

PIGLET CHRIS ENJOYS TAKING WAGON RIDES WHILE LEN FEEDS HIM A STEADY STREAM OF CHEERIOS.

WARNING: TO AVOID SERIOUS INJURY
inflating tires above 25 psi.
ual pump is recommended to prevent over inflation

AVERTISSEMENT: POUR ÉVITER LA BLESSURE SÉRIEUSE
mas gonfler de pneu au-dessus de 25 psi.
impe manuelle est recommandée pour empêcher par-dessus l'inflation

AS CHRIS GROWS, HE
CAN BARELY SQUEEZE
INTO HIS WAGON.

using red stretchy tape. He grabbed his camera and shot a video to share with a few friends on YouTube.

Len's friends started sharing *Pig in Wheelchair,* and the YouTube video skyrocketed him into becoming an Internet sensation. Chris P. Bacon and his wheelchair rolled into viewers' hearts all over the world. Soon the social media star had his own Facebook, Pinterest, and Twitter pages, along with a public relations manager and lawyer. Everyone wanted to meet the adorable pink pig. "People found him to be both unique and inspiring," Len explained. "I think viewers appreciated that he was given a second chance and had the option to be mobile in spite of his disability."

In the video, Chris snarfed up Cheerios and guzzled formula from a baby bottle. He smacked his lips and gobbled . . . like a pig! And soon he grew and grew, both in length and width. When Chris grew too big for his first toy wheelchair, Len built a second wheelchair, which the expanding pig quickly outgrew.

It was time for an upgrade. Len checked out a small dog wheelchair at a vet conference. When he showed Chris's video to the manufacturer, HandicappedPets.com donated the wheelchair, which could be adjusted as the pig packed on pounds.

Chris P. Bacon hit the ground running as soon as Len strapped him into his new blue wheelchair. He zoomed around the farm, chasing his best buddy, Aspen the border collie, and rooting around the yard searching for tasty treats. "When he's in his wheels, he acts like a normal pig," said Len, who also pulls Chris around in a Radio Flyer wagon.

And, oh, the places where this pig has traveled! He's been a special guest at children's hospitals and appeared at charity and veterans' events to support people with disabilities. On one memorable trip Chris flew to Boston. There he hammed it up for an audience at Franciscan Hospital for Children. Most

CHRIS NOSHES ON CEREAL TREATS WHILE ENJOYING A PANORAMIC VIEW WITH LEN.

of the young patients were amazed when the sensational swine rolled into the visitors' room, navigating through the crowd in a wheelchair.

Chris made the hospital rounds, demonstrating how he had overcome his physical challenges. He entertained the crowd with a repertoire of tricks, which included giving kisses. The kids greeted their special visitor with mile-wide smiles. According to Len, "Children in wheelchairs are especially interested in meeting Chris because they find something in common with him as soon as they see him." The pig hasn't stopped spreading his message: If you put your mind to anything, you can accomplish it!

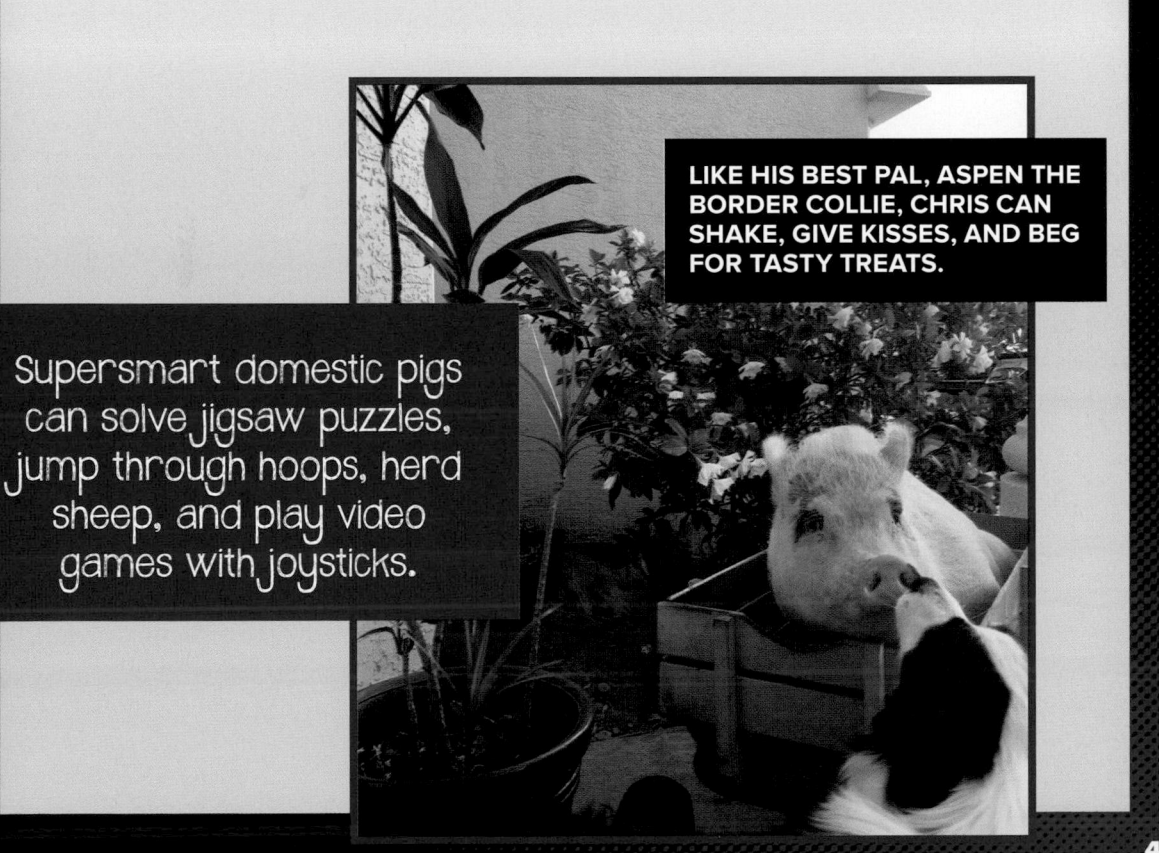

LIKE HIS BEST PAL, ASPEN THE BORDER COLLIE, CHRIS CAN SHAKE, GIVE KISSES, AND BEG FOR TASTY TREATS.

Supersmart domestic pigs can solve jigsaw puzzles, jump through hoops, herd sheep, and play video games with joysticks.

INGENIOUS SOLUTIONS

Need to solve a pet's mobility problem quickly? Get creative with household items! Chris P. Bacon zoomed around in a piggy wheelchair made of K'Nex construction toys, and puppy TurboRoo's first cart was assembled from a Fisher-Price helicopter, PVC pipes, and a ferret harness. Lily the lamb's quad wheelchair was also constructed from PVC pipes and caster wheels, with a sling sewn into it. Hoppy the goose skates on a child's Rollerblade, while the Pekin duck Lemon glides on a scooter made of PVC piping. Blue, Pablo, and Rolie, who are chickens, push themselves around on wire plant baskets mounted on wheeled planter casters. The African tortoise Gamera rolls on a swiveling wheel glued to his shell, and Arava, another African tortoise, uses a two-wheeled skateboard strapped to her shell. Blade the tortoise glides on a customized Lego skate glued to his shell, and Allison, the green sea turtle, gets clamped into her ninja suit thanks to a snowboard binding. A floating goldfish wheelchair was created from a bandage that acts as a harness and is attached to a cork to keep the fish stable and afloat.

HELPING PATIENTS TAKE STEPS TOWARD RECOVERY

When curious young patients peeked out of their hospital rooms, they were amazed to see a rabbit racing down the hallway. But the bunny with the spiky mane wasn't hopping. Instead, she was zooming around on a special scooter.

Alyna, a lionhead rabbit, was born paralyzed from the waist down. However, according to the physical therapist Riki Yahalom Arbel, the feisty bunny "was very motivated," dragging her hind legs to grab goodies out of the vegetable bowl.

Soon Alyna joined Riki at ALYN, a children's medical center in Israel. There this therapy rabbit acted as a role model for disabled children. Riki asked the lab to make a brace similar to what paralyzed children wear to assist their mobility. The rabbit-size version wrapped around Alyna's waist and legs. Thanks to spinning wheels, the bunny could scoot forward.

At first, Alyna struggled with her scooter just like the young patients, who found their braces scary and uncomfortable. But after a few days

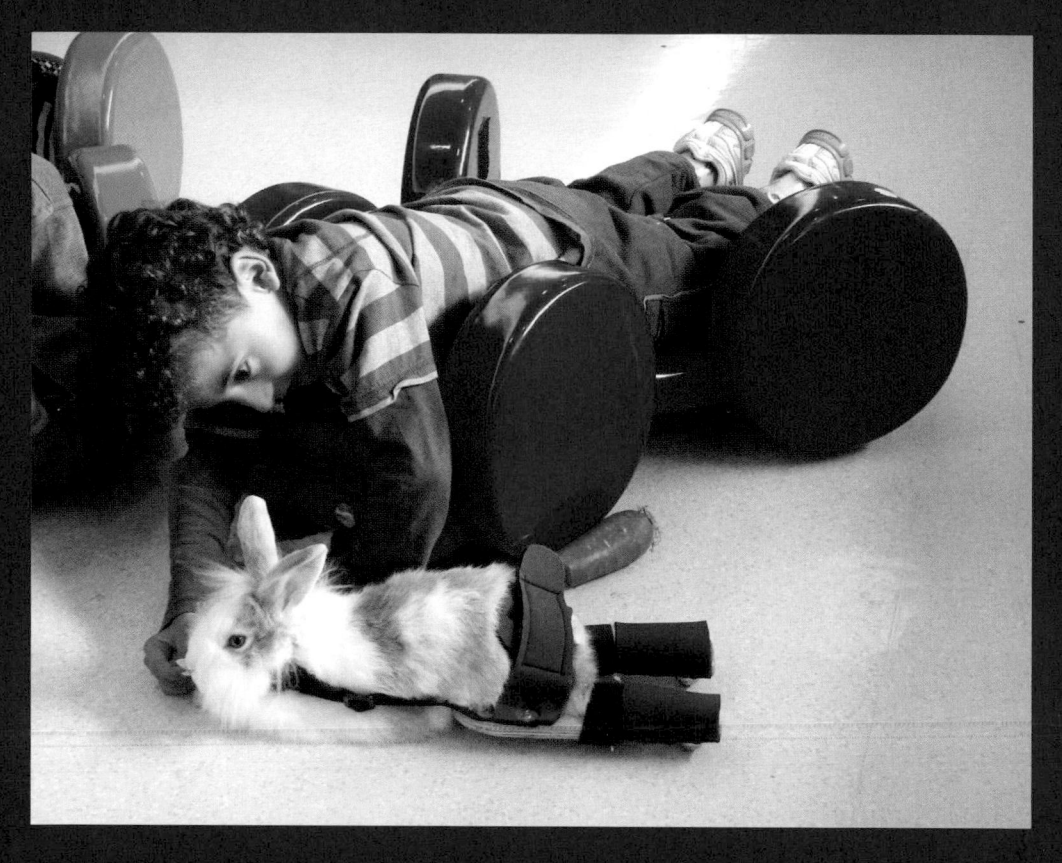

this rabbit was on a roll. "Once she realized that finally she could get anywhere she wanted, and much faster, she enjoyed it," Riki said.

Next Alyna accompanied Riki on her rounds for rehabilitation treatments. The children helped their physical therapist put the brace on the bunny. "They saw that she didn't like it, but they also saw how much it helped her," said Riki. Alyna provided positive reinforcement for mobility -challenged patients. The kids focused on the rabbit's capabilities, not her limitations.

Before long, Alyna had a fan club that snowballed into hundreds of young patients. Following the bunny's can-do lead, the children put on their braces each morning, then roamed the halls, searching for Alyna by following the sound of her wheels.

ESTELLA

A Rolling Rodent Rocks a Mini-Wheelchair

Estella curled up in her tiny fleece bed, listless and likely frustrated as she watched her pal Pip jumping with joy. Pip raced backward and forward and then repeatedly bounced into the air like a kernel of popcorn bursting from a hot pan. Guinea pigs do this hip-hop dance when they're in a playful mood.

Tiny two-pound Estella, a former pet, couldn't join in the fun. Her back legs didn't work. Someone had abandoned her and her constant companion, Pip, in a carrying case on the side of a rural road in the heart of the California Gold Country. Neighbors later divulged that a small child had squeezed the guinea pig, breaking her back.

Thanks to a Good Samaritan, the guinea pig duo ended up in an animal shelter; however, owing to a soaring homeless pet population in their area, Estella languished in a cage, with no vet care or pain medication for a month. Then a shelter volunteer reached out to Harvest Home Animal Sanctuary, a rescue and rehabilitation haven for mistreated companion and farm animals. Might they have a spot for Estella and Pip?

ESTELLA AND HER SIDEKICK PIP ARE NEARLY INSEPARABLE.

The sanctuary enthusiastically welcomed the two swirly-furred Abyssinian guinea pigs. Straight away, "Estella was examined by our veterinarian and given the much-needed pain relief she deserved," said Christine Morrissey, the sanctuary manager. The veterinarian confirmed that the guinea pig had permanent paralysis of her lower body and that surgery would not help her regain mobility.

The staff at the animal sanctuary brainstormed a way to improve the orange and white guinea pig's quality of life. They watched as a determined Estella dragged herself around using her upper body. There had to be a better way. An Internet search brought up Doggon' Wheels, and despite the name, the company *did* design and build wheelchairs for a variety of pets, including guinea pigs!

Harvest Home, like most animal sanctuaries, runs on a shoe-string budget. The sanctuary posted a plea for donations on Facebook, and Estella's wheelchair fund quickly met its $500 goal: $300 for the wheelchair and $200 for medical expenses. Then the guinea pig, who was the smallest resident at the sanc-tuary, got measured for her new wheels. The wheelchair, Chris-tine pointed out, "was designed as an exercise mechanism to increase her enrichment and activity level."

ESTELLA IS ON A ROLL IN HER MINUSCULE WHEELCHAIR.

And with Pip's encouragement, plus strawberry and grape treats for motivation, Estella now spends her time rocking and rolling in her wheelchair. The energetic and vocal guinea pig has gone from being treated like a piece of garbage left on the roadside to starring as the sanctuary's "treasured comeback kid," said Christine. "We are so inspired by her relentless resiliency."

ESTELLA LOVES HAVING CHILDREN READ TO HER.

Estella and Pip work together as a team, squeaking and squealing when they want the sanctuary staff to feed them more snacks.

HUDSON

Paying It Forward as a Top Therapy Dog

A prosthetic paw didn't stop Hudson from strutting down the red carpet at the Hero Dog Awards ceremony in Hollywood. However, the pit bull's exuberant personality proved to be an obstacle. "All Hudson wanted to do was say hello to all the photographers and give them his puppy kisses," recalled the pooch's best pal, Rich Nash. When the attention hound finally reached the stage, the American Humane Association crowned him the top therapy dog for 2015.

Hudson is a natural at lifting spirits when he volunteers with hospice patients and visits schools, kids' camps, hospitals, and recovery centers for amputees. The therapy dog's trademarks are his infectious grin and whirligig tail. To everyone he meets, Hudson happily demonstrates the motto for kindness that Rich created for him: "Just because you're different, you are still special in your own 'wooftastic' way."

The pit bull is so optimistic, it's difficult to imagine that his message might never have been broadcast. When Hudson and his two sisters were three weeks old, a cruel person nailed their paws to the railroad tracks in Albany, New York. Railroad workers saved the "railroad puppies," as they were dubbed, but Hudson's back paw needed to be amputated.

HUDSON VISITS SCHOOLS TO SHARE HIS SPECIAL MESSAGE, WHICH RICH CREATED FOR HIM.

The dog's surgeon recalled hearing about a cutting-edge technology for animals, and soon three-month-old Hudson became one of the first dogs in New York to receive a prosthetic limb. He was up and running on his new paw, chasing his sister right away. As Hudson grew to his full size, he went through approximately twenty paws.

The pooch "test drives" various prototypes for the prosthetic company Animal Orthocare, which has donated all the paws.

Derrick Campana, certified orthotist, designs all the paws by "first casting Hudson's leg to make a mold, then hand-sculpting the mold to prep it for fabrication. Plastics and foams are vacuum formed over the leg to truly customize the prosthesis. Last to be attached is the foot section, which is made from aluminum and shock-absorbing components to give it the spring needed to help Hudson walk better and more comfortably." Today the pit bull's stash includes four prostheses: one everyday paw, one "event" paw for special occasions, and two backups, just in case.

Along with all his "Blade Runner" paws, Hudson gained a family and an entire community. Rich and his wife, Rosemarie, saw a news story about the railroad puppies and their tragic beginning. Hundreds of other

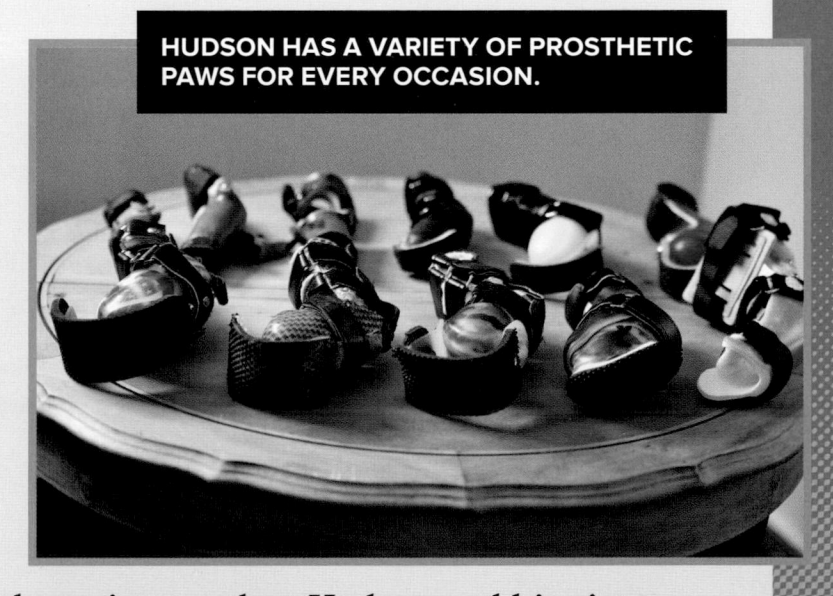

HUDSON HAS A VARIETY OF PROSTHETIC PAWS FOR EVERY OCCASION.

people did as well, clamoring to adopt Hudson and his sister Pearl (sadly, their smallest sister didn't survive). The humane society where the pups were sheltered decided that potential adopters should submit an essay explaining why their home was best suited for one of the puppies.

Rich and Rosemarie's essay emphasized how they were both self-employed and would be able to take their new puppy to any vet appointments or events on a moment's notice. Many people also contacted the shelter, putting in a good word for Hudson's potential "parents." After their essay won, Hudson joined his new family, which included another rescued pit bull, Sami, and five cats. The community rallied around Hudson with "an outpouring of love and support," Rich said. They cheered Hudson's

HUDSON HAS FANS OF ALL AGES!

victories, as did the more than twenty thousand fans on the dog's Facebook page.

Despite his *ruff* start in life, Hudson adores people. According to his family, the pooch is "a big love bug" who "is changing hearts and minds about the pit bull breeds one at a time." And Hudson has inspired his humans to "paw it forward" by advocating for tougher animal cruelty laws, such as the New York State animal abuser registry, which would identify convicted animal abusers so they cannot buy or adopt companion animals.

"When we adopted Hudson, we became his voice," said Rich.

HUDSON INSPIRES RICH AND OTHERS TO PAW IT FORWARD.

The pit bull was America's patriotic pup during World War I, starring on posters used to sell war bonds and recruit for the U.S. military.

MOLLY

Leaving Smiles Wherever She Goes

When Hurricane Katrina slammed into the Gulf Coast in August 2005, it triggered a catastrophic aftermath for both humans and animals, including an Appaloosa pony named Molly. Her humans had fled the storm, and massive flooding prevented them from returning to their barn. Thankfully, Kaye Harris and her husband, Glenn, arrived on the scene to rescue Molly along with other animals.

Molly's former family relinquished her to the Harrises, and the gray speckled pony settled into their Louisiana farm. Unfortunately, one of the dogs they rescued attacked Molly and severely crushed her right lower leg. Molly had survived one of America's worst disasters, but would she survive on only three legs?

Kaye believed that this pony wasn't ready to give up. Molly initially adapted to navigating on three legs. The smart pony shifted her weight while standing and even preferred to lie down on a hill so she could easily get up later. Horses pose an extreme challenge for prosthetic intervention because of their size; however, without a prosthetic, the healthy legs would eventually become injured because they would have to support more weight.

Still, the spunky pony showed a strong will to survive, and she had Kaye's loving guidance. Kaye invited Dr. Rustin Moore at the Louisiana State University School of Veterinary Medicine to meet Molly. The veterinarian agreed that she would be the "perfect candidate" for a prosthetic leg because the pony cooperated with her care. In a rare surgery, Dr. Moore amputated Molly's leg below the knee and fitted her with a hollow cast with a pole, which would act as her temporary leg.

Molly overcame the incredible odds: her operation was an outstanding success. As soon as she awoke, "she stood up and walked off," said Kaye, who cried tears of joy. "I knew it was going to work."

After Molly's stump healed, Dwayne Mara at Bayou Orthotic and Prosthetic Center built his first animal limb. He got down on his hands and knees to examine Molly's anatomy as she walked. Then he calculated what percentage of weight the leg would need to support. Molly was "timid and pretty easy to work with," Dwayne recalled, but his pony patient hated her first leg. It was too hot; when Molly's vet removed the leg, it was dripping with sweat, and the pony refused to allow it back on. So Dwayne went back to the drawing board, creating a silver and black leg that ended in a rubber hoof embossed with a smiley face. Molly gave it her stamp of approval!

KAYE HELPS MOLLY PUT ON HER NEW LEG, WHICH HAS A SMILEY FACE EMBOSSED IN THE RUBBER HOOF.

Most days Molly wears her prosthetic leg, but sometimes she displays a stubborn streak. If she doesn't want to wear it, "she'll pull up her stump and run away," said Kaye, adding that Molly is now on her seventh prosthetic leg.

Two years ago Molly got a special surprise: her own swimming pool! The soothing water massage helps prevent her body from twisting further. But how can a pony access an aboveground swimming pool? Kaye's husband and son devised a clever solution: they rigged up a zip line so Molly can be hoisted up in her sling and propelled into the pool for her half-hour massage.

Besides leaving a trail of smiley faces in the dirt, Molly also leaves smiles on people's faces. The pony's mission is to give back to the community by "spreading hope, love, cheer, and courage to those who need it," explained Kaye. Her cheerful pony adores visiting patients at children's hospitals and nursing homes, kids at schools and cancer camps, and soldiers at Walter Reed National Military Medical Center. Molly is living proof that "it's not about what you can't do—it's about what you can!"

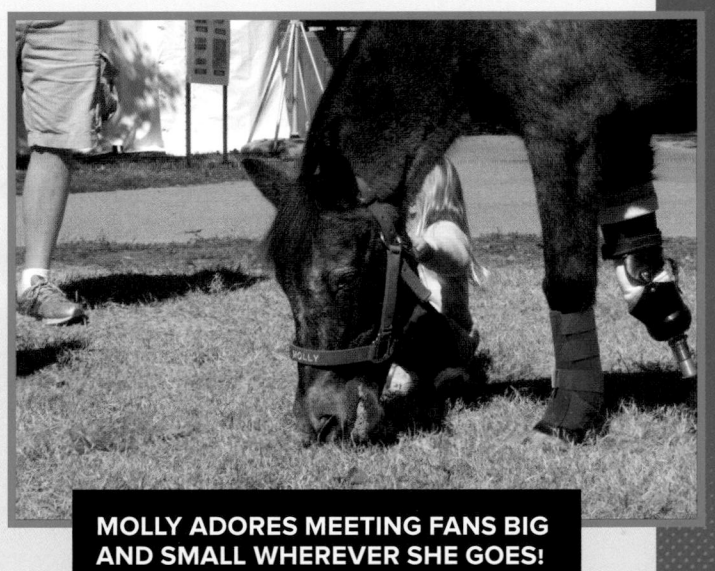

MOLLY ADORES MEETING FANS BIG AND SMALL WHEREVER SHE GOES!

Now that Molly is a senior, she receives healing alternative treatments: acupuncture, laser, and essential oils.

STROLLING TOWARD RECOVERY ON BOTH LEGS

"Fore!" a golfer should have yelled to alert about an oncoming golf ball. Unfortunately, the wayward shot struck a sandhill crane in his lower leg as he strolled across the Canadian golf course.

For days the tall gray bird with the crimson cap evaded capture until a wildlife biologist lured him with grain. Next, Dr. Ken Macquisten attempted to set the shattered leg, but the break was so bad that the vet had to amputate.

The crane "was a good candidate for a prosthetic device because of his personality," explained the wildlife rehabilitator Elizabeth Melnick. Sandhill cranes are a rare sight in Vancouver, but because Bunker, as he was soon named, was born on the golf course, he acted friendly.

It's a good thing the big bird enjoyed humans, as his recovery depended on several. First up, the vet improvised a makeshift prosthetic out of a wooden dowel. Bunker balanced on his new leg and took

BUNKER NEEDED A PROSTHETIC LEG AFTER GETTING HIT BY AN ERRANT GOLF BALL.

a few tentative steps. However, Bunker would need a sturdier leg if he wanted to perform the graceful dance sandhill cranes use to court the ladies.

Fortunately, OrthoPets heard about the bird and ensured that Bunker would have a full dance card. They crafted a plastic prosthetic leg after receiving a mold of the crane's stump. As soon as his new leg was snapped into place, Bunker started shaking his feathers and strutting around.

AFTER BUNKER'S NEW LEG IS SNAPPED INTO PLACE, THE SANDHILL CRANE STARTS STRUTTING AROUND WITH HIS HEAD HELD HIGH.

Then he convalesced at Elizabeth's Wildlife Center, gobbling the medicine she hid in blueberries. Once Bunker healed, the plan was to release him back into the wild, but the crane snuck out of a conservation center and vanished. If Bunker ventures near the golf course, everyone hopes he's learned to duck when he hears "Fore!" warning.

MR. STUBBS

Swimming Like an Olympic Champ

Splash! An orange floatie bobbed to the swimming pool's surface. A few seconds later an enormous green tail followed. That three-foot-long tail belongs to Mr. Stubbs, but it isn't the one he had when he hatched. Instead, this American alligator sports a scaly tail made of silicone.

His new prosthetic tail helped Mr. Stubbs learn to swim all over again. The floatie hugged his tail to stop him from sinking, but soon the determined alligator would ditch this inflated water wing. Every day Mr. Stubbs practiced his swimming lessons so he could propel through the water using his bionic tail.

Tails are vital appendages for alligators. Without tails, these prehistoric reptiles can't balance in their watery homes and are in danger of drowning. In 2005, when Arizona

MR. STUBBS TEMPORARILY USES AN ORANGE FLOATIE TO TEACH HIM TO SWIM WITH HIS NEW TAIL.

authorities discovered Mr. Stubbs crammed in the back of a truck with thirty-one other alligators intended as illegal pets, the young alligator was already tailless. A bigger, hungry gator had chomped off his tail for a snack.

Fortunately, Mr. Stubbs's story made waves. The gator got a second chance when the Phoenix Herpetological Society rescued him. There, the society president Russ Johnson and his staff gave the formerly bullied reptile special attention so he wouldn't always be last in the chow line. When it came time to swim, Russ recalled that Mr. Stubbs helplessly turned upside down and capsized, so he taught the alligator how to doggy paddle using his front legs. However, since "the tail is the main source of locomotion," Russ witnessed how the alligator could not swim "swiftly and naturally."

Mr. Stubbs needed a tail to turn his life around. In order to keep his body balanced, the tail would have to be designed with perfect proportions so that the growing gator would be able to move in the water and on land. A dream team of scientists, doctors for humans, and researchers tackled the challenge of fitting Mr. Stubbs with the world's first prosthetic alligator tail.

A bit of movie magic started the process. Dr. Justin Georgi of Midwestern University stuck reflective dots all over Mr. Stubbs. Then he used special infrared video cameras to track the gator's motion as he walked. This was "the same type of system that movie studios use to record the movements of actors for 3D digital special effects," Justin said.

Computer data from the camera sessions showed that most of Mr. Stubbs's problems "were related to improper posture. His hips were too high off the ground because his back legs were pushing with enough strength to carry a big, heavy tail, but the tail wasn't there, so his legs were pushing too much and in the wrong directions," Justin said. The weight of the prosthetic tail would be crucial, allowing the alligator's strong back legs to support "the right amount of body."

More movie magic helped a team design the perfect tail in multiple steps. First, Dr. Marc Jacofsky of the CORE Institute, a center for orthopedic research, took a mold of Mr. Stubbs's rear using flexible silicone, called Body Double, which the movie industry uses to create such special effects as masks and creatures' faces. Then he made an exact copy of the alligator's rear and designed a socket to fit his stump. "Making a mold was easier to work with than having a live alligator in the lab!" Marc said. Next, he found an alligator carcass with a tail that was approximately the correct size for Mr. Stubbs, and he made a replica using Dragon Skin, a soft yet super-strong silicone rubber that special effects artists use to create zombie makeup. Finally, Marc connected

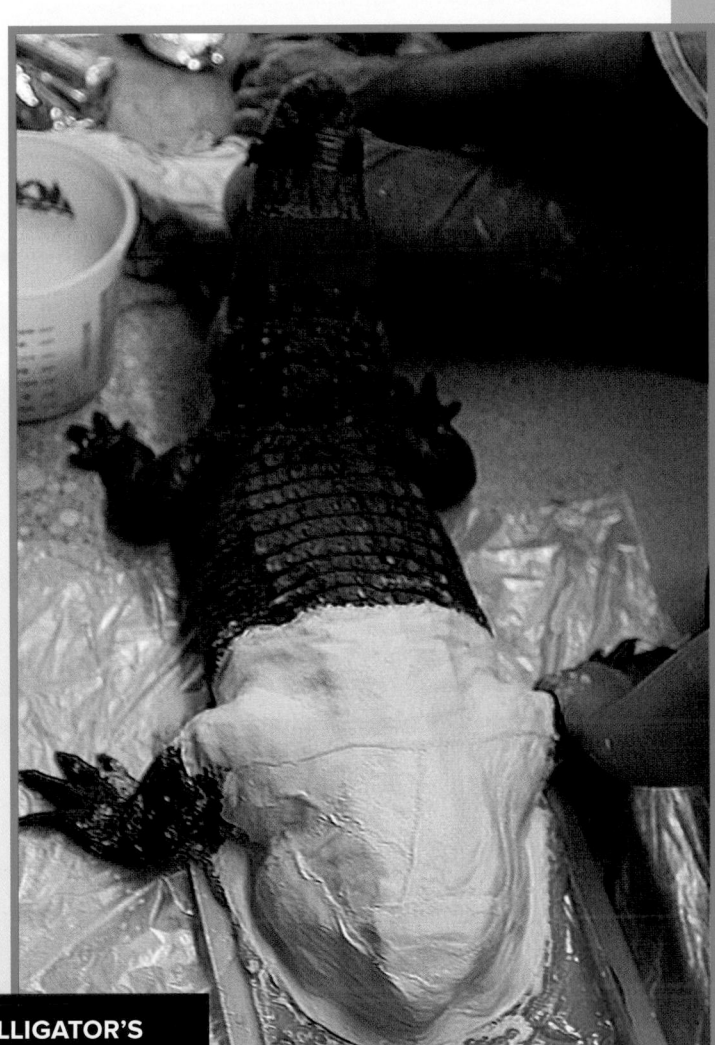

TAKING A MOLD OF THE ALLIGATOR'S REAR USING BODY DOUBLE SILICONE CONSTITUTES ONE OF THE MANY STEPS USED TO DESIGN A NEW TAIL.

the donor tail copy to the socket and harnessed it to the alligator's rear legs. Success—Mr. Stubbs finally had his tail!

Now the alligator faced a huge hurdle: unlearning the doggy paddle and using his thirty-five-pound artificial tail to swim. Russ Johnson gently placed his foot on the gator's back to hold him at the bottom of the pool, "forcing him to use the muscles in his hips and remnant tail." Those muscle memories sprang into action, and since then, Mr. Stubbs has been swimming like an Olympic champ, wiggling his hips and waving his brand-new tail.

As Mr. Stubbs continues to grow during his anticipated eighty-five-year life span, he will need up to twenty replacement tails, each costing around $6,000.

MR. STUBBS MODELS THE WORLD'S FIRST ALLIGATOR PROSTHETIC TAIL.

A DOLPHIN'S GEL HELPS HUMANS SLIP INTO PROSTHETICS

Human medical innovations often jump across the species barrier. Today dental braces and chemotherapy benefit our dogs and cats along with humans. But sometimes the opposite occurs, and a new veterinary invention can solve human problems. When an Atlantic bottle-nosed dolphin named Winter lost her tail in a crab-trap line, prosthetists designed her an anatomically correct tail.

Next they faced a challenge: how to keep Winter's new tail on her slippery, sensitive skin. Together with a chemical engineer, her prosthetists created a super-stretchy rubbery sock to grip the dolphin's skin and hold her new tail in place. Now this thermoplastic elastomer gel is helping human amputees.

AN ANATOMICALLY CORRECT TAIL HELPS WINTER TO SOAR THROUGH THE WATER.

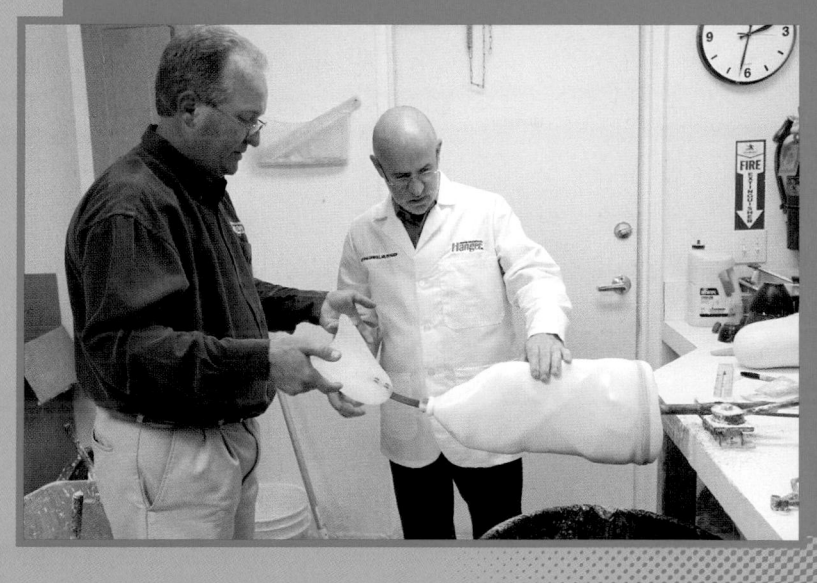

WintersGel Prosthetic Liners allow patients to comfortably wear prosthetics, whether they walk or swim, making an enormous difference in their lives.

TRIPOD

Walking with a New Spring in His Step

Two llamas on the lam, one with banana-shaped ears, frolicked through a Colorado paddock in a lively game of follow the leader. Close on their tail, two ranchers attempted to herd the independent-minded creatures into their horse trailer. Sherry Hughes and Marc Field of the Lazy Rocker Ranch, after discovering that their neighbor could no longer care for the pair, wanted the llamas to join their herd. But the llamas weren't ready to give up their eighty acres of freedom, and the ranchers left empty-handed.

The next day, they returned and finally cornered both llamas in a barn. The victory turned bittersweet when the ranchers scrutinized the white llama, who was sprinkled with brown freckles. "What looked like a piece of weed flapping under the llama's belly turned out to be the bottom portion of his leg," Sherry recalled. The broken hind leg hung on by skin and fiber (as llama "hair" is known).

The couple rushed the llama to their vet. Because the break was straight across, the vet guessed that the llama must have stepped into a hole, and the clean break meant that he was a good candidate for amputation. Soon a surgeon at the Veterinary Teaching Hospital at Colorado State University removed the leg below the hock, or the lower leg joint. If an animal's leg is amputated at the hip or shoulder, a prosthetic leg cannot be attached to a limb that isn't there, whereas a prosthesis can be used on a patient with a functional limb of appropriate length.

Sherry and Marc named the funny-eared young llama Tripod. In a stroke of good fortune, at a recent conference their vet had met a young man who'd started an unusual company in his garage. Martin Kaufmann had launched OrthoPets in order to craft prosthetics for animals.

Martin visited the barn to observe how Tripod moved and to scrutinize the physiology of the llama's three remaining legs. "I used the same techniques I would have used for a large human with a below-knee amputation," Martin recalled.

When Tripod was fitted with his first prosthetic, "he immediately took off, romping on it," Sherry said. But the exuberant llama forgot how to put the brakes on. He zoomed around a sharp corner, hooked his new rubber foot on a fence panel, and bent his metal leg supports at a ninety-degree angle.

On to Plan B. The ranchers hauled Tripod to OrthoPets so that Martin could design a leg and tweak changes all in one visit. This time Martin crafted a socket prosthetic specifically designed to withstand any antics a rambunctious quadruped could dream up. The updated prosthetic slips over the llama's leg stub, which is cradled in a rubber cup. Three Velcro bands encircle and support Tripod's upper leg. A high-strength aluminum extension leg reaches to the ground, ending in a rubber foot that's treaded like a tire to allow the llama to turn, spin, and walk normally.

TRIPOD'S PROSTHETIC LEG WITHSTANDS ANY MISCHIEF THE RAMBUNCTIOUS LLAMA GETS INTO.

TRIPOD'S HIGH-TECH LEG PUTS A NEW SPRING IN THE LLAMA'S STEP.

These days Tripod is on his fifth prosthetic leg. "He's very hard on them in his day-to-day living," Sherry pointed out. At the Lazy Rocker Ranch, Tripod cavorts with a herd of thirty-one rescued llamas and alpacas. His high-tech leg has given the happy llama a new spring in his step.

Guard llamas can protect livestock and poultry from predators by sounding an alarm call, spitting, and charging headfirst to chase the enemy away.

VINCENT

Moving Forward
on Titanium Legs

The tiny abandoned kitten desperately needed help to get back on his feet. Vincent struggled in vain to walk. Both of his hind limbs were missing from the mid-tibia, or shinbone, down. Had he already used up all of his nine lives?

Something about the plucky domestic shorthaired kitten captivated a worker at the humane society in Iowa where Vincent was surrendered. She brought Vincent home, and as soon as her daughter, a veterinary student, spotted the kitty, she had a brainstorm. Vincent should go to college! The daughter was certain that her instructor at Iowa State University could help the kitten.

At the university, Dr. Mary Sarah Bergh, associate professor of orthopedic surgery, took steps to tackle Vincent's dilemma.

"He could not walk or use his hind legs like a normal cat and could barely bend his left stifle [knee] at all," she observed. Neither physical therapy nor a wheelchair helped Vincent. It was time to consider a bold new plan, a cutting-edge procedure so rare that it had been performed on fewer than twenty-five animals worldwide.

One of those animals was Oscar, a British farm cat who'd tangled with a combine harvester and lost his back paws. Rather than prostheses that strapped or buckled on, Oscar received bionic feet implants known as endoprostheses. In a groundbreaking operation, the vet Noel Fitzpatrick, star of the documentary TV show *The Bionic Vet,* inserted metal implants into Oscar's ankles, where they fused with the bones. Then he attached bladelike artificial paws.

Endoprostheses also offered hope for Vincent, even though Mary considered this technology as "a last resort. It's expensive, not guaranteed to work, nor is it something that is easily undone." She worked with BioMedtrix, a leading veterinary implant manufacturer, to formulate custom implants for the kitten. They used x-rays and CAT scans to evaluate the size and shape of Vincent's bones, and then they created 3D model implants to rehearse the surgical procedure. To complicate matters, the team needed to create two separate designs because Vincent's femurs, or thighbones, where the implants would be placed, were two different sizes and shapes.

At first Vincent looked like a miniature peg-legged pirate. His short leg attachments were secured to the titanium posts that exited from his femurs. As soon as Vincent grew and built up muscle and bone strength, his legs could be lengthened by sliding longer attachments onto the posts.

VINCENT IS ONE OF APPROXIMATELY 25 ANIMALS WORLDWIDE TO HAVE PROSTHETICS IMPLANTED STRAIGHT INTO THE BONE.

Soon it was time for Vincent to take his first steps. "I was really surprised at how easily he adapted to the implants, because I wasn't sure he would know how to use his back legs in a walking fashion, since he had never been able to do that," Mary said.

Is there anything that this miracle kitty can't do? Vincent hasn't mastered jumping or racing up the stairs . . . yet.

DR. MARY SARAH BERGH EXAMINES VINCENT'S REVOLUTIONARY TITANIUM PROSTHETICS.

Vincent's custom-designed implants, donated by a veterinarian orthopedics company, would typically cost thousands of dollars.

FROM CLUNKY TO CUTTING-EDGE

For centuries, artificial limbs were crafted from wood and metal, and pirates weren't the only ones who relied on wooden peg legs and hook-shaped hands. These clunky replacement limbs offered basic functionality, but were overdue for improvement.

Today, cutting-edge prosthetics made of carbon fiber and plastic composites are built to be lightweight, strong, and durable, but not necessarily realistic-looking (think of the sprinting blades worn by disabled athletes who compete in the Paralympic Games). One female amputee, when challenged by a coworker, even built a prosthetic leg out of colorful Legos, although the foot snapped off because it lacked the range of motion necessary for walking.

Animal prosthetics are a twenty-first-century phenomenon. Their technology mimics that of human devices. Two types offer humans and animals support and natural movement. The first, known as socket prostheses, slip over the limb stump; straps, belts, buckles, and sleeves secure them into place. Sometimes a snug fit is created by suction alone, relying on an airtight seal to secure the limb in place. The second type, revolutionary integrated prostheses, are connected directly to the endoskeleton. One end of a titanium device is implanted in the bone. Then another removable part, such as a foot, is anchored in the device using a screw. This alternative method of attaching a prosthetic limb is a promising treatment for animal amputees. It has many advantages, especially ease of donning and doffing. However, it also has disadvantages, such as higher cost and longer rehabilitation time. This evolving technology should present exciting possibilities in the future.

THE TAIL END

Back at the Woodstock Farm Sanctuary, Felix the sheep pranced on his 3D-printed leg while Fawn the Jersey cow proudly marched around wearing just one pink leg brace. But what about Albie? The goat had kicked off his last prosthetic leg, so it was time to get rolling, literally, with something new: a specially designed front-wheel cart!

Albie uses three legs to propel through the pasture on his two-wheeled cart. His new wheels "allow him great mobility and ease the weight-bearing on his other front leg," said Jenny, who still hopes that Albie will walk on four legs someday. "Another prosthetist is currently working on another version of an artificial limb for him. It's been a prob-lem we eventually aim to solve!"

Albie, Felix, and Fawn inspire everyone who visits Woodstock Farm Sanctuary. Thanks to modern technology along with lots of love and support, this trio perseveres despite life's challenges. "They live life the way they were intended to live," said Jenny. "We're all about making sure these lucky animals have the best lives imaginable. There's no greater joy."

"Providing devices for disabled farm animals shows people that these animals are more than worthy of our moral consideration and deserve the same love and treatment we would provide to our beloved cats and dogs."

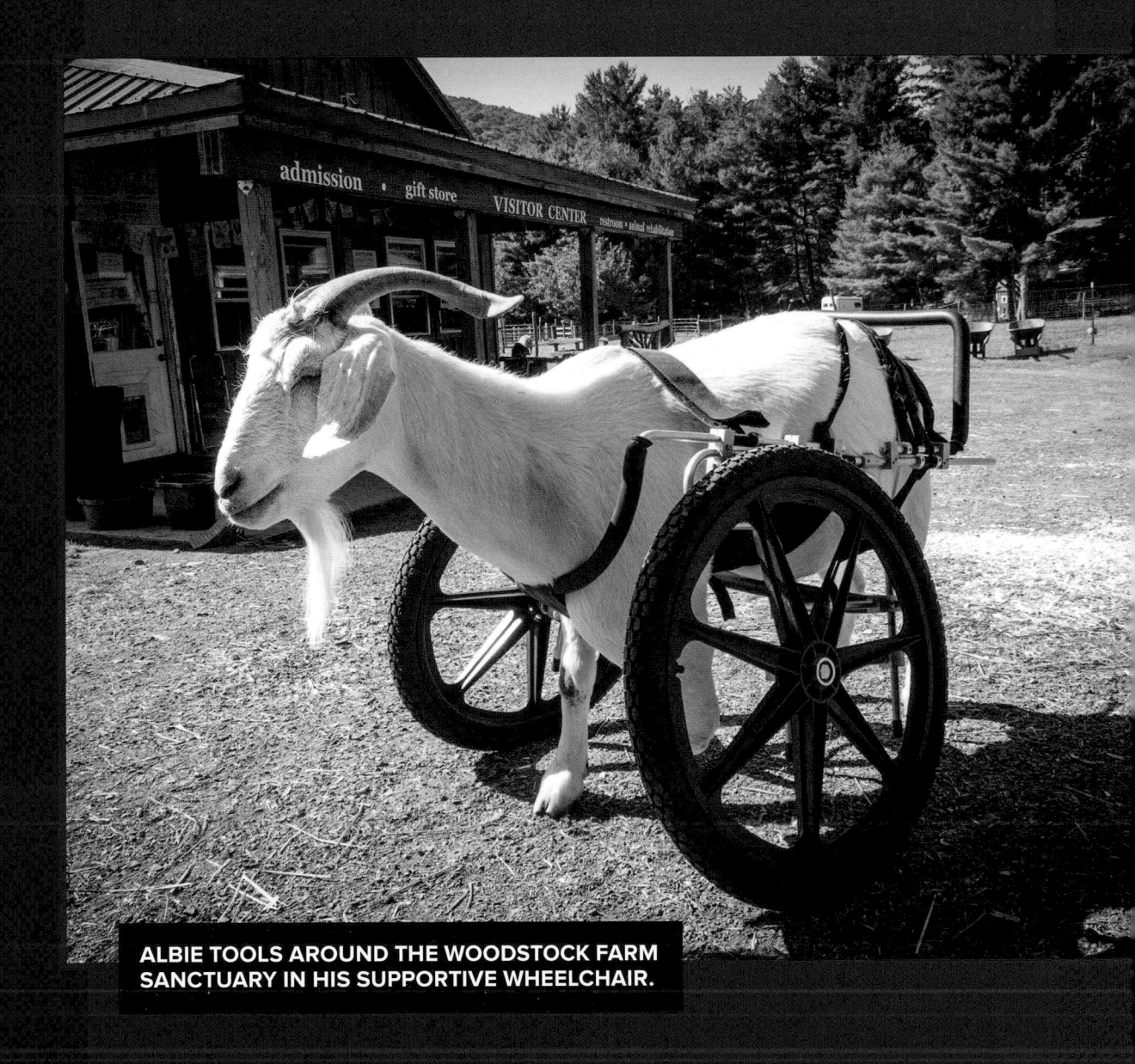

ALBIE TOOLS AROUND THE WOODSTOCK FARM SANCTUARY IN HIS SUPPORTIVE WHEELCHAIR.

THE WIZARDS
OF PROSTHETICS

JEFF COLLINS

K-9 Orthotics & Prosthetics

A poorly fitted and badly constructed prosthetic leg spurred a new career. When Jeff Collins wore his artificial limb, he experienced both frustration and discomfort. Although he did not yet have training in the prosthetics field, he decided to take action: he built his own leg.

Quickly realizing that he had an ability to help others in a similar situation, he trained to become a registered prosthetic technician. He specialized in fitting babies and toddlers with prosthetics. Because they were too young to answer questions or follow directions, these patients needed an expert who could intuitively help them.

Later Jeff used his skills in a similar way to help his dog Stash, who had torn a ligament in her knee. The only option at that time was surgery, yet he knew that humans who sustained the same injury would be given a knee brace. This solution didn't exist for dogs, so another idea flickered in Jeff's head, driving him to develop a canine product "based on the same physical principles as human braces."

Stash's brace, or orthotic, led to another breakthrough for Jeff: he started K-9 Orthotics & Prosthetics in 2004. Based in Nova Scotia, Canada, his company fits dogs—ranging from three pounds to two hundred—with braces, wheelchairs, and prosthetics. Dogs who have injured or damaged a leg, usually due to a torn ligament or arthritis, are candidates for braces, which can either help heal or stabilize the leg and allow for comfortable walking. A wheelchair lets a paralyzed dog become mobile; it also can help dogs learn to use their legs to walk again after accidents.

Dogs who are missing a portion of their limbs can use a prosthetic, but Jeff emphasizes that a stump is

K-9 ORTHOTICS & PROSTHETICS CAN HELP DOGS SUCH AS THIS NEWFOUNDLAND JEFF IS HOLDING.

necessary to hold the artificial limb in place while supporting the dog's body weight. First, Jeff takes a negative cast of the stump, filling this mold with plaster of Paris to create a positive cast, on which he builds the prosthesis. Next, he shapes foam over the positive cast to create a soft foam liner. Then he creates a plastic mold over the liner, using resin and carbon fiber materials to make a rigid plastic leg. Finally, he trims the edges to make them smooth and then adds straps and a paw with a rocker bottom sole "to create a leg that will roll forward smoothly when the dog is walking."

Along with providing patients with better mobility, Jeff has tackled some tough challenges. When a vet removed the lower jaw of a dog suffering from cancer, Jeff created a shell to take the place of the jaw and shield the dog's tongue, which "was hanging down and unprotected." This technological marvel allowed the dog to drink on her own again. He has also fabricated helmets for blind dogs. These contain a "rod looped in front that acts like a 'white cane' for the sight impaired so they don't run into anything."

Although Jeff specializes in canines, as reflected in his company's name, he's also worked with other species, including cats, alpacas, llamas, rabbits, and a moose calf. His most unusual case was a tortoise with a broken leg; he fabricated a wheelchair that could be adjusted as the reptile grew.

All these creatures seem to know that their medical devices were built to help them.

According to Jeff, even dogs who are considered power chewers rarely chomp on their braces. "They quickly recognize the support and benefit they receive from these devices," he said. Some of Jeff's four-legged patients even fetch their ambulatory devices and beg their humans to put them on so they can go for walks!

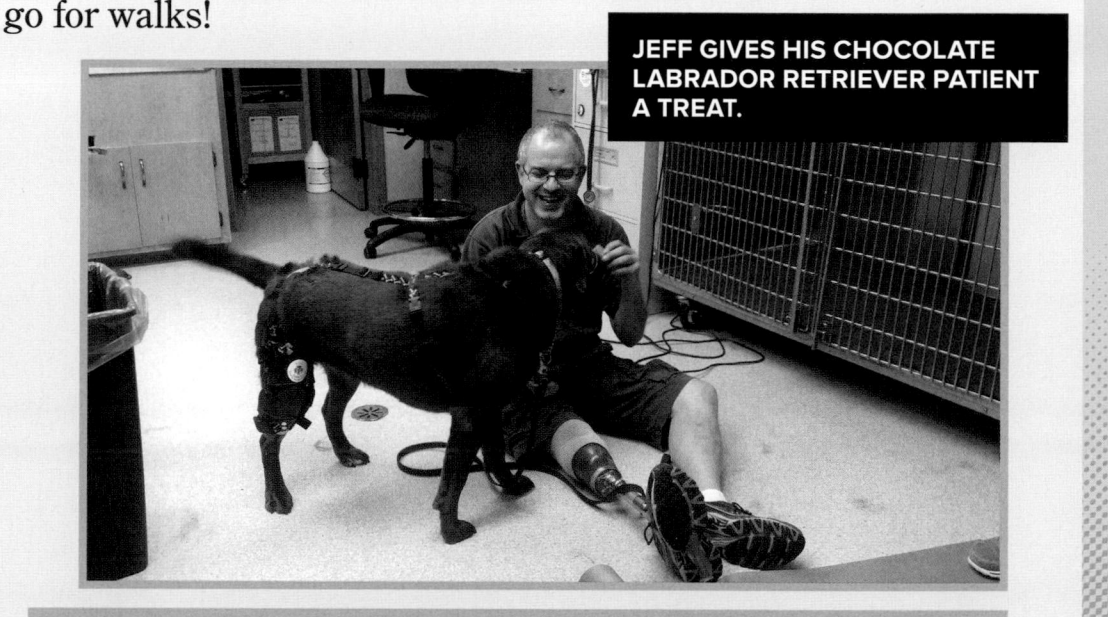

JEFF GIVES HIS CHOCOLATE LABRADOR RETRIEVER PATIENT A TREAT.

"We love our animals so much that we figured out how to help dogs who have the same kind of mobility problems that humans experience."

RONNIE N. GRAVES

Veterinary Inclusive Prosthetics/Orthotics

The logo for Ronnie N. Graves's website is "Experiencing Life . . . One Step at a Time." That describes both Ronnie and his animal clients. The owner of Veterinary Inclusive Prosthetics/Orthotics, based in Bushnell, Florida, has had an eclectic career that took him one step closer to his specialty: a prosthetist for large animals.

Ronnie lost one of his legs in an accident involving four train cars. By overcoming physical adversity, the former truck driver gained insight into the challenges faced by animals. "Being told what I can and can't do because I'm an amputee drives me to prove others wrong," Ronnie explained. "Wearing a leg gives me a feeling of what it's like to figure things out so I can do the things I want. It helps me design devices to enable the animals rather than disable them further."

Although he has nineteen years of experience crafting custom orthotics and prosthetics for many animals, Ronnie has migrated toward large farm animals. A neighbor who "begged" Ronnie to help her horse, Scarlet, spurred him to focus on "doing the impossible with large animals."

One of these animals is Luigi, a miniature Sicilian donkey with luminous chocolate eyes. Ronnie sent a specially built truck and trailer along with two employees up to Central New England Equine Rescue in Massachusetts to bring Luigi to his home in Florida. There he created a leg, along with two leg braces, for the donkey, who was born

RONNIE'S PET DONKEY, LUIGI, HAS A SUPPLY OF LEGS IN EVERY COLOR OF THE RAINBOW.

with part of his front left leg missing. Ronnie and his wife adopted Luigi so he could get a lifetime supply of legs crafted in a variety of colors. These days the donkey races through the pasture with Casper, his mule buddy, even rearing up and pawing the air! "Everybody deserves a chance, and he proves it every day," Ronnie said.

Perhaps Ronnie's most challenging case involved a Hereford steer named Dudley. After his leg became entangled in baling twine, Dudley's foot fell off. Thankfully, the cattle rancher spared the young male calf from the slaughterhouse and after nearly a year relinquished him to the Gentle Barn in Tennessee, a sanctuary for rescued animals. Dudley needed his damaged bone and muscle surgically amputated before Ronnie could design and build a new foot—a "very difficult" process for a thousand-pound animal. "I had to rethink the composite materials to create his socket," Ronnie explained.

An eager vet wanted Dudley to wear his new foot twenty-three hours a day, "but any new amputee takes a while, requiring a very slow, methodical process." The calf needed to acclimate to his new foot, with time off so air could recirculate and allow the skin to rebound, Ronnie explained. "Animals can't verbally tell us how it feels, so we have to listen with our eyes and observe their body language." After physical therapy on an underwater treadmill, acupuncture for pain, and chiropractic adjustments to straighten his spine, Dudley trotted off to join his bovine family at the Gentle Barn.

Ronnie handcrafts all his animal prosthetics. The first step is to create a mold of the leg. Then he figures out what type of padding to add. "Using liquid epoxy resin, I create a rigid socket for the prosthetic. A lot of math and engineering goes into this process."

RONNIE HANDCRAFTS A VARIETY OF PROSTHETICS AT HIS WORKBENCH.

Although he specializes in farm animals, the prosthetics maker has crafted body parts for household pets, such as dogs and cats. He even gave Hoppy the goose a bionic Rollerblade leg! The bird had no leg to attach to, so Ronnie scanned her underbody into a computer and used the scan to create her shape. Next he formed a thin shell with epoxy resin and fiberglass, and he used bolts to attach this to a child's Rollerblade. Her new leg was lightweight and waterproof, and it rolled like a wheelchair, so Hoppy could swim and spin anywhere she wanted.

Ronnie continues to strive to help all his feathered and furry patients. "Animals deserve an opportunity to enjoy life also, even if it means living that life differently from others," he said.

"The finest candidates for prosthetic limbs are the animals who have human caregivers who can devote the time needed to help them learn how to walk again. It's very rare to simply put one on and have them walk or run right away."

MARTIN KAUFMANN

OrthoPets

It's no coincidence that the letters "h-o-p-e" appear in the middle of the name OrthoPets. Martin Kaufmann, founder of the world's largest veterinary orthotic and prosthetic company, has been inspiring hope in animal guardians since 2003, when he launched OrthoPets in his four-hundred-square-foot garage.

Martin was working in the field of human orthotics when his cousin's schnauzer, Walt, suffered a stroke and was unable to use his front leg. "I knew I had to try something before they amputated the leg," he said. Walt's vet had recommended amputation, but Martin came up with a less drastic solution, even though, at that time, "it was unheard of for a pet to be fitted for a prosthesis or orthosis."

Martin used his imagination and skill to create a brace so

that Walt could walk on all four legs. Several versions later, after much trial and error, Martin had a new career: making veterinary orthotics and prosthetics. "I took the knowledge of the fabrication process and advanced biomechanics from the field of human orthotics and prosthetics and adapted these to four-legged patients," he said.

After working on animals exclusively since 2007, Martin said that he could not imagine going back to fabricating devices for humans. Each month, the Denver-based OrthoPets, which Martin runs with his wife, Amy, fabricates some two hundred custom-made orthotic and prosthetic devices for animals around the world. About 15 percent are prostheses. Martin's

patients have ranged from pet dogs to the more exotic, including a baby orangutan.

OrthoPets has the same goal for all species—to help their animal patients stay active and pain-free. However, this rewarding challenge is achieved using methods that "vary wildly. What an owner needs for a golden retriever will be drastically different from what a zoo needs for a turkey vulture, despite both of these patients suffering from the exact same injury," Martin pointed out.

Despite the differences, OrthoPets custom crafts all prosthetics in a similar manner. Since four-legged patients rarely stay still long enough for veterinarians to digitally scan their limbs, the first step is to make a fiberglass impression. Once OrthoPets receives that impression, they scan it to create a 3D model, an exact duplicate of the residual stump. Next, a CAD (computer-aided design) system allows OrthoPets to digitally modify the limb "to create the shape and contours needed to accomplish the therapeutic goal intended for the patient." Then a machine carves an exact replica of the digitally sculpted pet's limb into a block of polyurethane foam, which is vacuum-formed with plastic. Finally, this plastic shell is furnished with

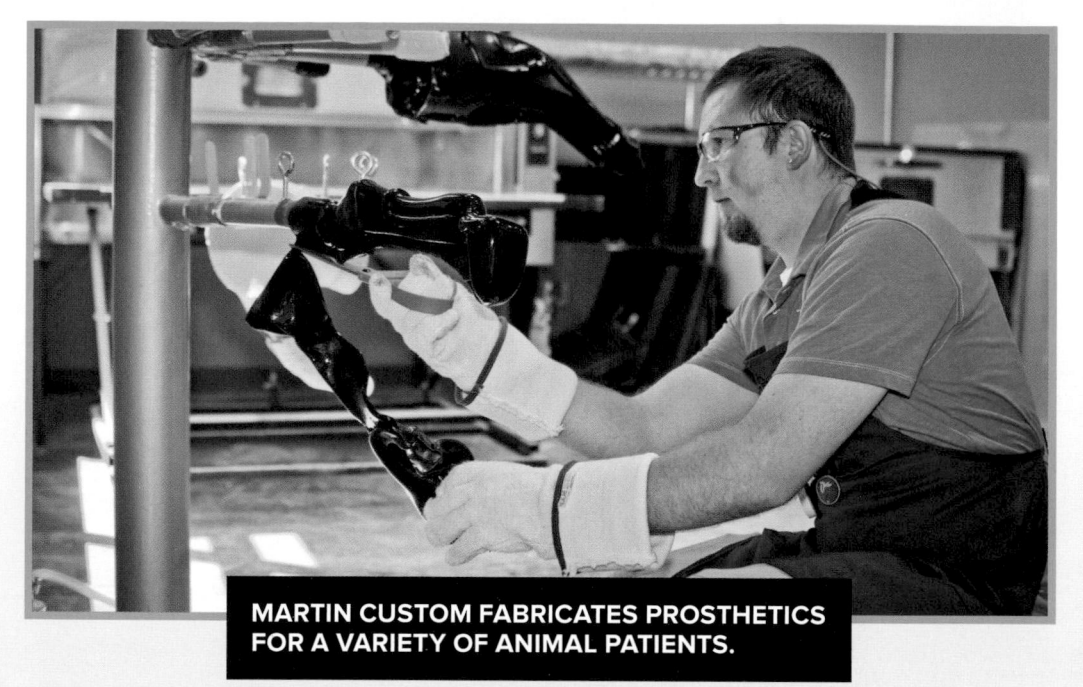

MARTIN CUSTOM FABRICATES PROSTHETICS FOR A VARIETY OF ANIMAL PATIENTS.

whatever is necessary to comfortably support the animal: hinges, pads, straps, and treads.

These amazing prosthetics provide animals a second chance to enjoy life. An animal might do fine on three legs, but as Martin emphasizes, an animal "could do awesome on four legs, whether one or all four are prosthetics."

Do prosthetics make animals happier? Absolutely, Martin says, observing that there's "a definite behavior shift" after an animal gains confidence and returns to normal. Against all odds, they have gone from being disabled to being enabled.

"All we need is a heartbeat and an appendage to help any species!"

"JUST LIKE ME!"

"Mom, she is just like me!" Averie Mitchell squealed with delight as she cuddled with the black Labrador mix puppy. The active nine-year-old girl was getting fitted for a new prosthetic leg. So was puppy Hattie Mae.

The two patients shared an instantaneous bond. Averie's right leg had been amputated seven years ago due to a rare shinbone condition. The lower part of Hattie's right rear leg was missing.

Neither Averie nor Hattie has let the loss of a leg slow her down. Averie competes in gymnastic events across Oklahoma and enjoys a variety of outdoor activities. Hattie is a joyous and playful puppy.

Each time Averie got fitted for a new leg, which involves taking a casted mold of her stump, the girl wiggled with excess energy. However,

AVERIE, A LEVEL 4 GYMNAST, PRACTICES A SPLIT ON THE BALANCE BEAM.

this time, according to Averie's mother, Kimberly, "Hattie laid her head in Averie's lap and they both sat there perfectly still. Averie immediately fell in love with Hattie; they were like a magnet to each other."

Fortunately, Hattie was searching for a new home, and the Mitchell family decided to adopt the pup from The Underdogs Rescue. The adoption has benefited both Hattie and Averie. "Hattie gives Averie confidence, and Averie loves showing Hattie new things," said Kimberly, adding that the two best friends love to play in the water and jump on the trampoline together.

Averie has big plans for Hattie. She wants to train the pooch to become a therapy dog. Then Averie can bring Hattie to hospitals "and show other kids that having an amputation isn't the end of the world."

AVERIE AND HER BEST PAL, HATTIE, ENJOY FUN ACTIVITIES BOTH IN AND OUT OF THE WATER.

AVERIE PLANS TO TRAIN HATTIE TO BECOME A THERAPY DOG SO SHE CAN PUT A POSITIVE SPIN ON PEOPLE AND PETS WHO'VE HAD A LIMB AMPUTATED.

A HELPING HAND

Have you seen children wearing colorful mechanical hands? These hands boost their confidence and even make them feel like superheroes. People around the world are using 3D printers to create prosthetic devices for kids in need—children who at one time could only dream of receiving a hand.

Instead of pricey, professionally made prosthetic hands, which can range from $6,000 to $10,000, the "DIY" versions cost between $20 and $50 for materials. And who won't want to wear a model called the Cyborg Beast or Raptor Hand? Amazing 3D printers can spit out a hand in about twenty hours; assembly requires two to three hours.

Invented in the 1980s, 3D printing technology creates solid objects from digital files. First you use a 3D scanner to make a copy of an object or a computer-aided design program to create a new object from scratch. Then special software prepares

THIS 3-D PRINTED STAR WARS BIONIC HAND WITH COOL FEATURES SUCH AS LED LIGHTS IS CRAFTED FOR KIDS.

your digital file for printing by "slicing" the object into horizontal layers. Next, the printer moves a nozzle in two directions to draw one layer at a time using threads of molten plastic. Finally, the object is formed layer by layer until it becomes three-dimensional.

Now 3D print technology is having a revolutionary impact on animals as well. Innovators created these ingenious solutions to transform animals' lives:

A bald eagle named Beauty received a bionic beak after a poacher shot off the top half of hers. Using 3D modeling and printing, a team designed an exact fit, right down to the sharp hook on her upper beak that allows Beauty to eat, drink, and preen her feathers.

BALD EAGLE BEAUTY BEFORE AND AFTER RECEIVING HER BIONIC BEAK.

Buttercup the duck, who hatched with a backwards-twisted foot, got a new silicone foot. A 3D printing company used photos of a duck pal's foot as a model, and now Buttercup has a foot with a bendable ankle and bottom tread.

BUTTERCUP THE DUCK CAN WADDLE AROUND THANKS TO HER NEW SILICONE FOOT.

The Leghorn chicken Cecily received a plastic leg to replace one of hers that had a damaged tendon. Veterinarians at Tufts University duplicated the chicken's healthy foot and made a $2,500 prosthetic plastic leg so that Cecily can comfortably roost.

CLEOPATRA THE LEOPARD TORTOISE SPORTS A BOLD RED CARAPACE DESIGNED BY A UNIVERSITY STUDENT.

Cleopatra, a leopard tortoise, had a deformed shell that had peaks and valleys, leaving her susceptible to infections, so a university design student spent six hundred hours creating a red plastic carapace for her.

Cyrano the cat got back on his feet when he received a replacement knee joint. After beating bone cancer, the kitty had difficulty walking until a miniature knee implant offered him the ability to move freely again.

The husky mix Derby, born with deformed front legs, sprints on loop-shaped legs. The special design allows the pooch to rock back and forth so he doesn't get stuck in the dirt.

Dudley the duckling tested out a selection of new legs after losing his leg in a fight with a flock of chickens. Dudley uses his flexible plastic leg to swim and waddle alongside his potbellied pig pal.

The box turtle Stumpy lost her injured leg to infection. A team of fifth-grade students created a 3D-printed ball caster that acts as a wheel, allowing the turtle to roll around.

TurboRoo, a homeless Chihuahua born with no front legs, found a family and a mission. A two-wheeled mobility cart created on a 3D printer allows the pooch to zoom around; now TurboRoo Designs offers carts for other two-legged pups.

A NOTE FROM THE AUTHOR

Two of my house rabbits sparked the idea for this book. LuLu Belle and Woody both hopped into my heart with their positive attitudes. There was no stopping LuLu Belle once she found her center of gravity. This Flemish giant bunny had the temperament (and silhouette) of a large-breed puppy. She was curious and affectionate, and her right rear leg was missing. After flunking

LULU BELLE, THE AUTHOR'S RESCUED FLEMISH GIANT TRIPOD RABBIT, SERPENTINES THROUGH THE YARD USING A UNIQUE LOCOMOTION PATTERN.

Fostering 101, I quickly discovered that LuLu Belle's confidence was as big as her impressive size. She even demonstrated lopsided binkies—

WOODY, ALSO ADOPTED BY THE AUTHOR, IS QUICKER ON THREE LEGS THAN MOST RABBITS ARE ON FOUR.

joyous bunny dances—to show off her exuberant personality. No one dared to call her disabled!

Later I adopted Woody, a Flemish mix who was missing his left rear leg. Although they didn't wear prosthetics or roll around in wheelchairs, both bunnies motivated me to persist despite challenges and obstacles that would have tossed up roadblocks in the past. Flash forward a few years, to when I researched hero dogs for *Paws of Courage*. I profiled two amazing tripod pooches in my book—Layka and Lucca—military working dogs injured overseas while sniffing out bombs. Both of these courageous canines quickly adjusted to life on three legs. Neither lost their speed or zest when they lost their front leg.

Suddenly I was meeting an amazing array of animals who lacked body parts, but not spirit. Some wore braces, like Layka, others had been fitted with replacement parts or wheelchairs, and a few bounced back to enjoying life on three legs. As I researched this book, new stories of brave bionic animals have made headlines. I was thrilled to profile a selection of species from around the world.

After reading this book, I hope readers will consider adopting or fostering an animal who is physically challenged. The joys are boundless!

GLOSSARY

carbon fiber (noun): an extremely strong and lightweight synthetic fiber.

endoprosthesis (noun, plural: *endoprostheses*): a prosthetic device that is placed within the body to replace a missing part.

orthosis (noun, plural: orthoses; from Greek *orthōsis,* "making straight"): an orthopedic device, such as a brace, that provides support or correct alignment.

prosthesis (noun, plural: *prostheses*; from ancient Greek *prósthesis*, "addition"): an artificial device, either external or implanted, that replaces a missing or injured body part. Along with the most typical limbs (arms and legs), the term can refer to fingers, toes, ears, eyes, and noses, along with paws, tails, beaks, and fins. The body part could be lost through congenital conditions, disease, or trauma.

prosthetic (adjective): relating to prostheses or artificial parts.

prosthetics (noun): the surgical specialty concerned with the design, construction, and fitting of prostheses.

prosthetist (noun): someone who specializes in the fabrication and fitting of prosthetic limbs. A prosthetist needs to be part inventor and part scientist, with a combination of anatomy, engineering, mathematics, and physiology (the mechanics of how living things function) skills. Two boards in the United States certify prosthetists: the American Board for Certification in Orthotics, Prosthetics and Pedorthics (ABC) and the Board of Certification/Accreditation (BOC). Both ABC and BOC require prosthetists to have a master's degree in orthotics and prosthetics and to complete a yearlong residency with a prosthetist before taking their board exams.

thermoplastic elastomer (noun): a mixture of polymers and rubber that combines the properties of both, such as flexibility with toughness.

vacuum formed (verb): a process in which a sheet of plastic is heated so it becomes flexible and then shaped by being placed in a mold while a vacuum pumps out the air beneath the plastic.

BIBLIOGRAPHY

Allan, Kate. *Oscar the Bionic Cat*. West Sussex, UK: Summersdale Publishers, 2013.

Anthes, Emily. *Frankenstein's Cat: Cuddling Up to Biotech's Brave New Beasts*. New York: Scientific American Books, 2013.

Clements, Isaac Perry. "How Prosthetic Limbs Work." How Stuff Works: Science, 2008. science.howstuffworks.com/prosthetic-limb.htm

Cook, Leslie. "3D Printed Animal Prosthetic Stories: Antidote to the News." 3D Universe, 2015. www.3duniverse.org/2015/04/15/3d-printed-animal-prosthetic-stories-antidote-to-the-news

Hatkoff, Craig, Isabella Craig, and Juliana Craig. *Winter's Tail: How One Little Dolphin Learned to Swim Again*. New York: Scholastic, 2009.

Hewitt, John. "The Future of Permanent, Fully Integrated Prosthetic Limbs and Bionic Implants." ExtremeTech, 2014. www.extremetech.com/extreme/189746-the-future-of-permanent-fully-integrated-prosthetic-limbs-and-bionic-implants

How Products Are Made. "Artificial Limb." Artificial Limb Forum. www.madehow.com/Volume-1/Artificial-Limb.html

Kaster, Pam. *Molly the Pony: A True Story*. Baton Rouge: Louisiana State University Press, 2008.

K-9 Orthotics & Prosthetics. www.k-9orthotics.com.

Mroz, Jacqueline. "Hand of a Superhero: 3-D Printing Prosthetic Hands That Are Anything but Ordinary." *New York Times*, February 16, 2015. www.nytimes.com/2015/02/17/science/hand-of-a-superhero.html?_r=0

"My Bionic Pet." *Nature* (PBS). DVD. 2014.

Norton, Kim M. "A Brief History of Prosthetics." Amputee Coalition: Limb Loss Resource Center. 2007. www.amputee-coalition.org/inmotion/nov_dec_07/history_prosthetics.html

OrthoPets. Orthopets.com

Rogers, Kara. "Animal Prosthetics: Surviving on Human Ingenuity and Compassion." Encyclopædia Britannica, February 22, 2010. advocacy.britannica.com/blog/advocacy/2010/02/animal-prosthetics-surviving-on-human-ingenuity-and-compassion

Veterinary Inclusive Prosthetics/Orthotics. my-vip.com

LEARN MORE ABOUT THE ANIMALS

Chris P. Bacon

www.chrispbacon.org

Harvest Home Animal Sanctuary (Estella)

harvesthomesanctuary.org

Iowa State University (Vincent)

www.news.iastate.edu/news/2015/12/02/vincentthecat

Kids and Ponies—Molly's Foundation

www.mollythepony.com

Phoenix Herpetological Society (Mr. Stubbs)

www.phoenixherp.com

Sea Turtle, Inc. (Allison)

www.seaturtleinc.org/rehabilitation/allison

Wildlife Alliance (Chhouk)

www.wildlifealliance.org

Woodstock Farm Sanctuary (Albie, Fawn, and Felix)

woodstocksanctuary.org

Many of the animals featured in this book have Facebook pages and YouTube videos.

PHOTO CREDITS

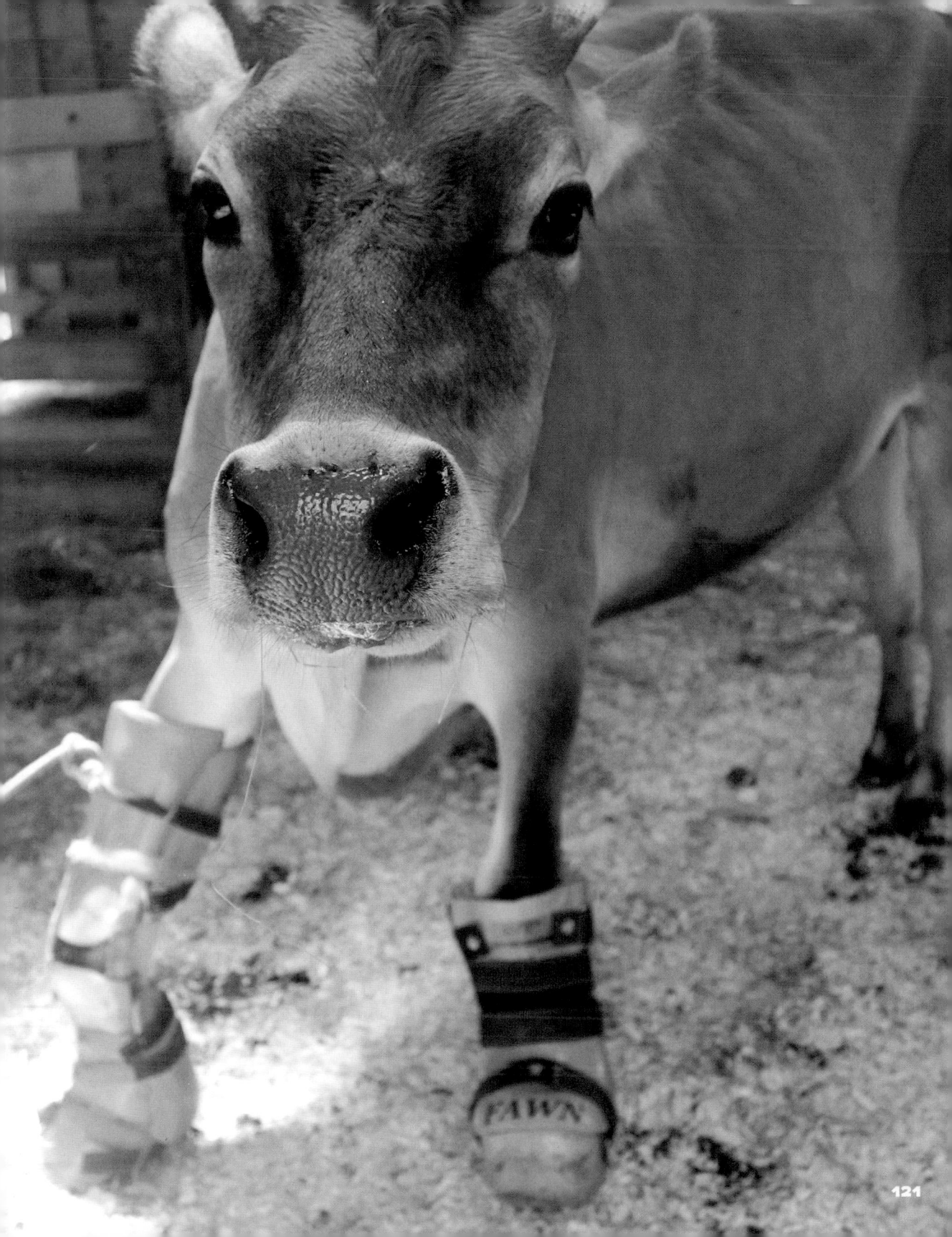

ACKNOWLEDGMENTS

Tail wags to my agent, John Rudolph.

Thanks to the invaluable editorial assistant Harriet Low.

Applause to all the creative folks at HMH.

Graphic gratitude to the designer
Andrea Miller for her fabulous talent.

Paws up to the animal-loving editor Erica Zappy Wainer,
who shepherded the manuscript with her incisive commentary.

INDEX